Understanding Foreign Direct Investment

Policy Studies Series

This series is designed to fill a visible gap in existing Social Sciences literature: the need to address, empirically investigate and rigorously analyse public policy in the field of governance.

It is important to study the policy world in its entirety because:

- Policies establish the context within which we live out our individual and collective lives, and deeply impact the way we and future generations will live and work.
- Policymaking and implementation is a process that is deeply embedded in politics, and serves as an entry point into the politics of a country.
- Public administrators, scholars, journalists and specialists need to understand the relationship between knowledge systems, technology and the making of policy, the nature of public participation and responses, and how politicians seek to forge networks to ensure that policy is transformed into law.
- Policymaking highlights the linkages between domestic and global contexts. Ideas disseminated through global institutions and civil society networks impact policymaking insofar as they influence identification of problems and propose resolutions.

The literature generated through the series, we hope, will serve to identify the strength and lacunae of the making of policy and its implementation in India.

Understanding Foreign Direct Investment

Biswajit Dhar
K. S. Chalapati Rao

Orient BlackSwan

UNDERSTANDING FOREIGN DIRECT INVESTMENT

ORIENT BLACKSWAN PRIVATE LIMITED

Registered Office
3-6-752 Himayatnagar, Hyderabad 500 029, Telangana, India
e-mail: centraloffice@orientblackswan.com

Other Offices
Bengaluru, Bhopal, Chennai, Guwahati,
Hyderabad, Jaipur, Kolkata, Lucknow, Mumbai,
New Delhi, Noida, Patna, Visakhapatnam

First published by Orient Blackswan Private Limited 2020

ISBN 978-93-5287-989-2

Typeset in
ITC Berkeley Oldstyle Std 10.5/14
by Le Studio Graphique, Gurgaon 122 001

031673

Printed in India at
Akash Press, Delhi

Published by
Orient Blackswan Private Limited
3-6-752 Himayatnagar, Hyderabad 500 029, Telangana, India
e-mail: info@orientblackswan.com

Contents

Abbreviations

ADR	American depositary receipts
BIS	Bank for International Settlements
BIT	Bilateral investment treaty
BPM	Balance of Payments Manual
CAD	Current account deficit
CFP	Consolidated FDI Policy
CDIS	Coordinated Direct Investment Survey
CIFLA	Census of India's Foreign Liabilities and Assets
CMIE	Centre for Monitoring Indian Economy
DIPP	Department of Industrial Policy and Promotion
DPIIT	Department for Promotion of Industry and Internal Trade
DPN	Draft Press Note
ECB	External commercial borrowing
ESO	Employee stock option
EU	European Union
FCCB	Foreign currency convertible bonds
FCRC	Foreign-controlled rupee company
FDI	Foreign direct investment
FERA	Foreign Exchange Regulation Act
FII	Foreign institutional investment
FIPB	Foreign Investment Promotion Board
FPI	Foreign portfolio investment
FVCI	Foreign Venture Capital Investment

G-20	Group of Twenty
GAAR	General Anti-avoidance Rules
GDP	Gross domestic product
GDR	Global depositary receipt
IET	Interest equalisation tax
IMF	International Monetary Fund
IPO	Initial public offering
IPS	Industrial Policy Statement
IT	Information technology
LIBOR	London Interbank Offered Rate
NDA	National Democratic Alliance
NRI	Non-resident Indian
M&A	Merger and acquisition
MBRT	Multi-brand retail trading
MSME	Micro, small and medium enterprise
OCB	Overseas corporate body
OECD	Organisation for Economic Cooperation and Development
OPEC	Organisation of Petroleum Exporting Countries
PE	Private equity
R&D	Research and development
RBI	Reserve Bank of India
SAR	Special Administrative Region
SDR	Special drawing rights
SEBI	Securities and Exchange Board of India
SEZ	Special Economic Zone
SIA	Secretariat for Industrial Assistance
SNA	System of National Accounts
TMG	Technical Monitoring Group
TNC	Transnational corporation
UNCTAD	United Nations Conference on Trade and Development
UPA	United Progressive Alliance

Figures, Tables and Boxes

Figures

Tables

Boxes

Acknowledgements

Our academic collaboration began more than three decades back at the Corporate Studies Group of the Indian Institute of Public Administration. In the subsequent decades, we continued to put our heads together at the Institute for Studies in Industrial Development (ISID) and Research and Information System for Developing Countries (RIS), the two institutes that gave us the opportunities and infrastructure to take our research interests forward.

We are extremely grateful to the management of ISID, in particular to Professor S. K. Goyal (vice-chairman) and Professor M. R. Murthy (director) for supporting us in every way to pursue our work. Sadly, the late chairman of the institute, Shri T. N. Chaturvedi, who was a constant source of encouragement, is not with us to see our endeavour come to fruition.

We would also thank our many well-wishers, especially Professor Muchkund Dubey, for inspiring us. And, finally, we would thank our wives, Apurba Moitra and K. Lakshmeeswari, for quietly motivating us.

Biswajit Dhar
K. S. Chalapati Rao

one

Foreign Direct Investment in the Post-decolonisation Era

Foreign direct investment (FDI) has been extensively discussed in the received literature through 'two related but [yet] different sets of topics or activities' (Lipsey 2001: 1), anchored in two very distinct traditions. The first of these deals with FDI as a component of finance, which influences the economies of both the home and the host countries of foreign investors. A section of the literature places FDI at par with development finance, for it is seen to plug the resource gap of host countries. The second tradition analyses many different facets of the principal organisational manifestation of FDI, namely the transnational corporations (TNCs). The behaviour of these firms, especially their motivations and the incentives to invest in foreign jurisdictions as well as their relationships with their home and host countries, is captured in a large body of literature. Broadly viewed, the former tradition is developed within the macroeconomic framework, while the latter is more centred in the microeconomic tradition and also borrows significantly from the institutional economics framework.

FDI as an important source of long-term finance has been analysed from the point of view of its implications on the macro-economy, especially its impact on the savings–investment situation and on balance of payments (Meier 1966: 471). Although this aspect of FDI inflows can impact both the recipients and providers of investment, the focus of much of the academic research has been on the former set of countries.

Available literature has argued that FDI inflows are essential for bridging the gaps between the investment needs and domestic resource mobilisation, typical of developing countries. In fact, this was the avowed objective with which the largest creditor country at the end of World War II, namely the United States, had defined its foreign policy from the late-1940s. The policy framework was put in place in 1949 by President Harry Truman through his 'Point Four' programme, the 'fourth point' in his foreign policy, which was to respond to the development needs of the under-developed countries.[1]

This chapter deals with two sets of issues. We begin by recalling the narrative on FDI that dominated the immediate post-World War II phase. The role of FDI in the context of development of the then underdeveloped regions was extensively discussed in this phase; we provide a flavour of the views that were expressed by some of the major contributors to the debate.

The second part of the chapter traces the evolution of FDI since the middle of the twentieth century. There are roughly four broad phases over which FDI has evolved. In the first phase, the first two decades following World War II, FDI flows were expectedly influenced by the policies adopted by the US, the only significant creditor country. Beginning with the 1950s, the US administration provided incentives to private investors from its territory to expand their global operations, including to the underdeveloped regions. From the early-1960s, the world's largest economy faced balance of payments difficulties stemming from the deficits on both the current account and the capital account. The US administration responded to its balance of payments difficulties by taking control of outflows of capital, which meant uncertain times for foreign investors. For private investors, these uncertainties of the 1960s not only remained, but were exacerbated in the following decade with the breakdown of the fixed exchange rate mechanism provided by the Bretton Woods system, and with it, the Gold Dollar Standard.[2]

In the second phase, which roughly corresponds to the breakdown of the Bretton Woods system in 1971, FDI became a relatively smaller player in global financial flows. This phase was dominated by bank finance that came into prominence through the recycling of petrodollars.

The third phase begins with the revival of FDI flows in the 1980s, after the onset of the external debt crisis of the developing countries. Large swathes of the developing world were saddled with a serious debt-overhang, caused by their over-exposure to the US banking system from the 1970s. With the debt-ridden countries facing serious constraints in financing their debt-service commitments, a case was made for injecting 'new money' into these economies. At least two supporting arguments were made for the infusion of FDI: the first was that FDI inflows were relatively more stable and predictable as compared to the debt-financed forms, and two, FDI inflows were non-debt creating and would hence not add to the payment liabilities of the recipients.

The fourth phase, from the early 1990s, coincides with the popularity gained by market-oriented reforms from the early-1990s. Liberalisation of FDI polices became an integral part of the reforms agenda. Over the three decades since then, therefore, governments have transformed themselves from 'quasi-regulators' of foreign investment[3] to outright facilitators.

Narratives on FDI in the Mid-twentieth Century

The years following World War II also coincided with the decolonisation of most of the present-day developing countries.

In discussions on the economic revival of these countries, FDI was considered as an important source of finance. One of the early proponents of this formulation was a group of experts appointed by the Secretary General of the United Nations (henceforth, the UN Expert Group) that was tasked with the responsibility of identifying the measures necessary for the economic development of the underdeveloped regions. The UN Expert Group estimated that the annual shortfall of savings over investment needs of underdeveloped countries would be about $14 billion if the national income of these countries were to grow by 2 per cent. According to the experts, this savings–investment gap had to be met through annual inflows of foreign capital of more than $10 billion (United Nations 1951: 79).

Ragnar Nurkse held a contrary view, arguing that foreign investment would not help in bridging this gap (Kattel, Kriegal and Reinhart 2011: 146). He argued that the demand for foreign investment was aplenty in underdeveloped countries, and that there were several supply-side bottlenecks. The key factor was that foreign investors lacked sufficient inducement to invest in these regions (ibid.: 120) Private investment, argued Nurkse, was influenced by market demand, which was too small in most of the developing countries to act as an incentive for foreign investors to invest in these countries. He argued that foreign investors were mainly interested in operations that can best be described as extension of the colonial pattern, namely investing in the production of primary commodities and in extractive industries in order to fuel the demand for these commodities in their home countries. They did not bring sizeable investments into any country unless they had necessary inducements.[4]

From the point of view of the recipient countries, FDI was particularly attractive. The attraction towards FDI lay in its three attributes discussed in the literature. The first is what Nurkse called 'real addition' to the productive capacities by FDI in the host countries (ibid.: 162). The second is that FDI is perceived as a more stable form of investment as compared to other forms, especially portfolio investment (Dutt 1998: 165). And the third is that FDI is not mere financial flow; it comes along with a 'package of intangibles', including technology and managerial skills. We will dwell on the last of these attributes in a later section.

While the necessity of foreign capital for addressing the problems of underdevelopment received uncritical acceptance, views were divided about the contribution that FDI could make in capital-deficient countries. The UN Expert Group alluded to two obstacles to the further expansion of FDI. First, several underdeveloped countries did not view this kind of investment very favourably, for they had fears about foreign control of important sectors of their economies. Second, the cost of foreign private capital was too high. For instance, the average rate of return on US foreign investments in 1948 was about 17 per cent, as compared to about 14 per cent on its domestic investments (United Nations 1951: 81).

Penrose (1956: 233) substantiated this view. She argued that intrinsic difficulties of controlling direct private investment once it was established, the problem of paying for it, together with the political fear of foreign 'exploitation' and domination, led many underdeveloped countries to explore ways of hiring foreign management and technical personnel, and purchasing access to foreign technology. In other words, these countries were not certain that FDI, as a 'package of intangibles', would be beneficial to them.

Hunter (1953) was somewhat more explicit in this context:

> foreign investors have not always acted in the best interests of the countries in which they have invested (or in their own best interests either), that the character of development and particularly its direction has not always been the most desirable, that rates of

> return have been too high in some cases, that labour has been exploited monopsonistically, that undue political influence has been assumed by investing firms, and that private investment has led to concentration of ownership of the factors of production to the exclusion of potential native operation. (Ibid.: 24)

He, therefore, pointed out that the task before underdeveloped countries was to decide 'how much correction of the evils of foreign investment can be accomplished without reducing its flow below the level necessary to produce given results' (ibid.).

Cardoso and Dornbusch (1989: 1413–14) provided a comprehensive list of problems they saw were associated with the activities of foreign companies, because of which commercial loans were preferred to FDI.

First, rather than help bridge the domestic savings and investment gaps in their host countries, foreign companies could lower savings and investment by not reinvesting their profits, and by backing groups whose propensity to save was low and propensity to import was high. Higher import-intensity of these companies meant that domestic companies did not get opportunities to expand.

Second, instead of closing the gap between investment and foreign exchange requirements in developing countries, foreign companies could reduce foreign exchange earnings in the long run. The current account could deteriorate due to increased import propensity of the foreign companies and repatriation on account of profits, interest, royalties and management fees.

Third, foreign companies could cause reduction of government revenues because host governments provided liberal tax concessions, investment allowances, disguised public subsidies and tariff protection.

Fourth, foreign companies could worsen income inequalities in their host countries by promoting the interests of a 'small number of well-paid, modern-sector workers' (ibid.), while ignoring most workers in the traditional sectors. The companies could divert resources away from the much-needed food production into the manufacture of sophisticated products consumed by the local elite.

Fifth, foreign companies could introduce in their host countries products that stimulate inappropriate consumption patterns through advertising, and use inappropriate technologies of production. This could lead to diversion of local resources into socially undesirable projects.

Sixth, the management, skills and overseas contacts provided by foreign companies could have little or no impact on local enterprises.

Seventh, the tendency of foreign companies to use transfer prices in intra-firm transactions could 'diverge from equivalent arm's length market prices that would be set in trade between unrelated parties' (ibid.). Under- or over-invoicing of exports or imports in order to shift profits, and evading taxes and foreign exchange controls, could be greater for intra-firm trade as compared to the trade between independent companies that are usually not given to these practices.

Finally, it is difficult to put an exact price on technology transfer, especially if technologies are transferred as one of the elements of a package of resources provided by FDI.

Evolution of Policies on FDI since the Mid-1940s

Policies on FDI in the immediate post-World War II decades were dictated by the largest and the only creditor country for most of the post-War years, namely the US. As the only economy of substance in the capitalist world, the US effectively dictated global capital flows.

Policies in the 1950s and 1960s

In the 1950s and 1960s, the US administration adopted two contrasting sets of policies. In the 1950s, the most significant of the policies adopted was President Truman's 'Point Four' initiative, a legislation[5] that was to assist the peoples of economically underdeveloped areas to raise their standards of living and encourage outflow of private investment beneficial to their economic development (Truman 1949a: 184).

One of the key features of Point Four was President Truman's emphasis that private investors must be encouraged to provide a major part of the capital required for American investment to the underdeveloped countries. The US administration also recognised the need to provide protection to American enterprises investing in underdeveloped countries, and suggested that entering into investment protection agreements with the recipient countries could be an option.[6] The administration pointed out that a major limitation of such agreements was that they were incapable of addressing problems relating to the inability of the underdeveloped countries to garner the foreign exchange necessary to service the investments. Under such circumstances, the possibilities of default by the recipient could be higher.

Table 1.1 captures the response of private investors to the policy measures taken by the Truman administration during the first decade of the implementation of the measures. The figures show the annual changes to the stock of US FDI abroad, which comprised the gross outflows of FDI and the reinvested earnings of the American companies in their host territories. These are the closest approximations of the inflows of FDI. Table 1.1 shows that as a result of the measures taken by the administration to promote long-term investment, annual increments to FDI steadily increased in the first half of the 1950s, before registering a quantum jump in the second half of the decade.

Table 1.1: US FDI Abroad, 1949–60

Year	*FDI Abroad ($ Billion)*
1949	1.1
1950	1.1
1951	1.3
1952	1.7
1953	1.4
1954	1.1
1955	2.0
1956	2.9
1957	3.1
1958	2.1
1959	2.4
1960	2.9

Source: *Survey of Current Business*, US Department of Commerce, various issues.

The destinations of FDI from the US remained mostly confined to the traditional partner-countries in the Americas (Table 1.2). Well above two-thirds of the investments went to Canada and Latin America until the mid-1950s. The underdeveloped regions, mostly in Africa and Asia, received a negligible share of the FDI. Thus, despite the emphasis of the Truman administration's 'Point Four' and the UN Expert Group's expectation that the resource gaps faced by the underdeveloped countries would be plugged by private foreign capital, companies were not very enthusiastic. Even after the US administration had offered to protect their investments in many of these newly independent countries through bilateral investment treaties (BITs), the companies chose to be dictated by their perceptions of commercial risks while dealing with the underdeveloped countries.

Table 1.2: US FDI: Share of Major Recipients, 1949–60 (%)

Year	Europe	Canada	Latin America	Middle-east Asia	Far-east Asia	Africa	Others
1949	18.2	63.6	45.5	n/a	n/a	n/a	–27.3
1950	18.2	45.5	9.1	n/a	n/a	n/a	27.3
1951	23.1	30.8	38.5	n/a	n/a	n/a	7.7
1952	5.9	29.4	35.3	n/a	n/a	n/a	29.4
1953	21.4	50.0	14.3	n/a	n/a	n/a	14.3
1954	18.2	54.5	18.2	n/a	n/a	n/a	9.1
1955	20.0	35.0	20.0	n/a	n/a	n/a	25.0
1956	17.2	34.5	17.2	n/a	n/a	n/a	31.0
1957	22.6	41.9	9.7	2.5	5.8	–0.1	17.6
1958	14.3	33.3	19.0	1.5	–24.1	4.5	51.4
1959	33.3	33.3	12.5	3.6	3.0	3.4	10.8
1960	82.8	27.6	10.3	–0.4	2.4	3.0	–25.7

Source: *Survey of Current Business*, US Department of Commerce, various issues.

The Tide Turns: US Controls on Foreign Investment Abroad

By the late-1950s, the US began feeling strains on its balance of payments, a problem that aggravated considerably soon after. The deterioration of the balance of payments occurred primarily due to three factors. First, US monetary reserves had suffered an unprecedented decline since the late-1940s. Second, the current-account balance had deteriorated, and third, net outflows of private foreign investment had increased, essentially due to increase in FDI outflows, which was the largest component of private capital outflows (Triffin 1966: 7).

FDI had increased from $7.8 billion in 1949 to $36 billion in 1964; the increase coming on the back of a four-fold increase in inflows in gross terms during this period. By the beginning of the 1960s, almost half of the global outward FDI flows were contributed by investors based in the US. No other country was anywhere close to making the contributions that investors from the US had made; the United Kingdom had the next largest share, at 18 per cent, and the Netherlands had 10 per cent (Lipsey 1999: 12).

The response of the US administration to the burgeoning capital-account deficit was to regulate outflows of foreign investment from the US. The first of these regulations was the interest equalisation tax (IET), which appeared on the statute books in 1964, but was made effective retroactively from the date the regulation was announced in July 1963. Using this instrument, the administration tried to make acquisition of fixed interest-bearing assets as well as foreign equities unattractive for American investors. IET had a major impact on the outflow of private portfolio capital into foreign securities (Strauber 1970: 10). Notwithstanding its impact, IET was unable to address the primary problem of leakage of funds through the capital account, owing to the relatively small share that portfolio investment had in the total private capital outflows from the US.

It was, therefore, hardly surprising that the US administration should have introduced a separate set of measures focusing on restricting FDI outflows. In 1965, the Voluntary Foreign Credit Restraint Programme introduced non-mandatory controls on direct investment abroad by American corporations and lending to foreigners by American commercial banks, which lasted until the end of 1967. The US Department of Commerce encouraged nearly 600 corporations responsible for the major share of FDI outflows to borrow abroad, to finance their investments in other countries. Further, they were asked to improve their contributions to the country's balance of payments by repatriating their short-term assets held abroad, increasing their exports and enhancing the remission of foreign earnings (Adler 1971: 3).

The non-mandatory controls failed to achieve the desired results in curbing outflows and improving the balance of payments position. This prompted the US administration to introduce mandatory controls on external operations of the corporations. The Foreign Direct Investment Regulations of 1968 were aimed at reducing FDI outflows by $1 billion from the level in 1967 (Willey 1970: 98).

The Regulations were applied to the 'direct investor', defined to include any entity which directly or indirectly owned or acquired (a) 10 per cent or more of the total voting power of any foreign entity; or (b) the right or power to receive, control or enjoy 10 per cent or more of the earnings, receipts, income or profits of any foreign entity; or (c) the right or power to receive, control or direct the disposition of 10 per cent or more of the assets of any foreign entity upon liquidation [Executive Order No. 11387 (1968) § 1000.304]. Identifying a 'direct investor' in this manner was an important step towards developing the norms for defining FDI, an issue we will dwell on in Chapter 2.

An official assessment of the outcome of the FDI Regulations was that there were no significant changes 'in the rate of accumulation of assets abroad' that could be attributed to FDI (Joint Economic Committee 1971: 43). In other words, the Regulations were unable to realise the immediate objective, namely curbing FDI outflows from the US by $1 billion between 1967 and 1968. Table 1.3 shows that the yearly changes in FDI maintained its upward trend in the medium term. The explanation for the later trend was that direct investors were 'able to carry out their plans while meeting the restrictions of the program because they ... made substantial amounts of foreign borrowings, usually in place of domestic borrowings' (ibid.).

The inevitability of failure stared at the Regulations as the US administration and corporations had sharply conflicting interests: while the former was concerned about the country's economic health, the latter were only interested in protecting their lucrative

Table 1.3: US FDI Abroad, 1961–70

Years	*FDI Abroad ($ Billion)*
1961	2.9
1962	2.5
1963	3.5
1964	3.7
1965	5.1
1966	2.3
1967	4.8
1968	5.3
1969	6.2
1970	7.4

Source: *Survey of Current Business*, US Department of Commerce, various issues.

international markets. Thus, the 1960s ended with the principal creditor country adopting a contrasting policy regime on FDI outflows, as compared to the one at the beginning of the decade: policies encouraging American corporations to invest abroad were replaced with a set of repressive policies. These policies also signalled the beginning of a period when the share of FDI in international capital flows declined.

Declining Role of FDI in the 1970s

Foreign capital inflows financed between 10–20 per cent of the total investment requirements of developing countries in the 1960s and 1970s. A bulk of these inflows originated from official or semi-official sources, and were either grants or concessional and non-concessional loans. Private finances were largely of suppliers' credits and FDI.

The global financial market turned on its head during 1973–75, when the first oil price shock sent the trade deficits of middle-income developing countries spiralling upwards, forcing these countries to borrow heavily. During these years, deficits of the oil-importing developing countries as a whole rose by more than three-fold in real terms, rising to 5 per cent of their gross domestic product (GDP) by 1975. The trade deficit of low-income countries increased somewhat slowly, by more than double in real terms during 1973–75. These countries were less affected since they were less dependent on oil.

FDI was about 20 per cent of the net capital inflows to the developing countries in 1970. This component grew relatively less as compared to the other forms of external capital during the 1970s, but in the early years of the decade, the situation was considerably different. A combination of commodity boom and favourable policies toward FDI adopted by the middle-income countries in Latin America from the late-1960s fuelled capital inflows. However, after 1975, money-centre banks' expansion and the consequent spike in commercial bank lending led to a change in the form of foreign investments in developing countries: intra-company loans supplanted equity participation. TNCs looked increasingly towards sources other than the parent company to meet their financing needs, which included borrowing from the private capital markets.

Among the components of foreign sources of finance, lending by commercial banks registered the highest growth, from nearly \$4.0 billion in 1970 to over \$36 billion in 1980. The banks had clearly emerged as the financial intermediaries by replacing governments and multilateral agencies as principal lenders to the developing countries. It must also be noted that bank lending to these countries was not without the 'encouragement and implicit support' of governments of the developed economies (Dooley 1994: 4).

While such inflows were critical for meeting the financing needs of developing countries, especially in view of the rapid deterioration in their trade deficits, the consequences of this magnitude of borrowing was felt acutely by the borrowers. By 1980, the outstanding debt of developing countries to private lenders had shot up to $284 billion, from $32 billion in 1970 (World Bank 1981: 52). Most of this increase was on account of the syndicated bank loans that had been taken on floating interest rates. When they had initially borrowed, the benchmark interest rate, namely the London Interbank Offered Rate (LIBOR), was lower than the rate of inflation, and this gave developing countries the advantage of accessing the funds, often at negative interest rates. But once the global economy entered the zone of uncertainty, and inflation raised its head, developed countries, especially the US, adopted tight monetary policies, the immediate impact of which was felt by the LIBOR. From 1977–78, oil-importing developing countries dipped into the international capital markets when the phase of negative real interest rates was well behind them. From then on, these countries were left to bear the heavy load of servicing the loans, and on increasingly adverse terms.

Table 1.4 provides the details of the current-account deficits experienced by developing countries in the 1970s and the sources financing their deficits. It also shows the drastically changing patterns of financing of deficits, especially for the middle-income countries. In relation to bank finance, FDI played a vastly diminished role in providing hard currency to these countries. This situation would change yet again in the 1980s, when the heavily indebted countries weathered the headwinds of rising indebtedness, and FDI was offered as a source of mitigating the problems.

Third-world Debt Crisis in the 1980s and FDI

FDI was back in favour as the preferred form of international finance, from the beginning of the 1980s (Table 1.5).

Table 1.4: Sources of Finance of Oil-importing Developing Countries, 1970–80 ($ Billion, in 1978 Prices)

Item	*Low-income Countries*					*Middle-income Countries*				
	1970	*1973*	*1975*	*1978*	*1980*	*1970*	*1973*	*1975*	*1978*	*1980*
Current-account deficit	3.6	4.9	7.0	5.1	9.1	14.9	6.7	42.8	20.4	48.9
Financed by net capital flows										
Official assistance	3.4	4.1	6.6	5.1	5.7	3.3	5.3	5.3	6.5	7.9
FDI	0.3	0.2	0.4	0.2	0.2	3.4	5.1	3.8	4.6	4.5
Commercial loans	0.5	0.6	0.8	0.9	0.7	8.9	13.7	21.0	29.4	27.1
Financed by changes in reserves and short-term borrowing*	–0.5	–1.1	–0.7	–1.1	2.4	–0.8	–11.7	12.7	–20.1	9.5

Note: *Minus signs (–) indicate increase in reserves.
Source: World Bank (1981: Table 5.1).

Table 1.5: Direct Foreign Investment in Selected Country Groups, 1965–83

Country Groups	*Average Annual Value of Flows ($ Billion)*			
	1965–69	*1970–74*	*1975–79*	*1980–83*
Industrial countries	5.2	11.0	18.4	31.3
Developing countries	1.2	2.8	6.6	13.4
Latin America and Caribbean	0.8	1.4	3.4	6.7
Africa	0.2	0.6	1.0	1.4
Asia, including Middle-east Asia	0.2	0.8	2.2	5.2
Other countries and estimated unreported flows	0.2	–1.0	0.6	4.8
Total	6.6	12.8	25.6	49.4

Source: World Bank (1985: Table 9.1).

FDI flows registered sharp increases in all regions except Africa as compared to the previous decades. In overall terms, there was a doubling of inflows between 1975–79 and 1980–83, a pattern that was seen particularly for all developing countries put together.

The trigger for a virtual metamorphosis of the global capital market was the oil price hike of 1973 that left a sizeable surplus of oil revenue with the oil-producing countries, cartelised as the Organisation of Petroleum Exporting Countries (OPEC). This surplus oil revenue, the so-called petrodollars, was first deposited in the banks in Western countries, and later reinvested in securities or other assets. Deposits placed in these banks between 1978 and 1982 accounted for 28 per cent of investable funds accumulated over the same period (McGuire and Tarashev 2006: 19). The net liabilities of the BIS-reporting banks to OPEC member states increased two-fold over this period, resulting in the OPEC countries becoming some of the largest net suppliers of funds to the international banking system.

The banks became lenders to the developing countries, and they did so with the approval and encouragement of the advanced-country governments (Dooley 1994: 3–4). The increase in bank lending took place also because commercial banks saw recycling as a profitable business. Increasing the legitimacy of the banks were the governments, especially the US government, which were not willing to extend to the developing countries either official credit or support-expansion of credit from the multilateral financial institutions, that is, the World Bank and International Monetary Fund (IMF) (ibid.: 4). Finding willing borrowers was not difficult throughout the Latin American region, since an excessively loose monetary policy followed by the Federal Reserve Bank of the US from the middle to the end of the 1970s fuelled the rate of inflation, resulting in the decrease in short-term real interest rates to close to or below zero (Feldstein 1991: 3).

Borrowers preferred to secure bank credit from the more traditional sources, as the banks were able to offer cheap credit for the reasons just stated. The behaviour of the banks was perfectly rational, for they felt assured that their losses could be shifted to the governments.

But by the beginning of the 1980s, the situation became adverse for both the borrowers and the lenders. The second oil price shock sent the inflation rate soaring and the US Federal Reserve Bank responded by raising the interest rates. The jump in the real interest rates caused an appreciation of the US dollar. Struck by the twin costs of higher interest rates and a higher value of the dollar, the sovereign borrowers declared insolvency, triggering the debt crisis (Table 1.6).

With bank finance, the largest component of private capital flows, imposing heavy liabilities on the developing country debtors and resulting in the most extensive sovereign debt default in history, search began for sources of foreign capital that could deliver on two counts: (a) allow the debt-stricken countries to grow out of their indebtedness and (b) prevent reoccurrence of a debt-induced crisis. Cardoso and Dornbusch (1989: 1434) argued that commercial banks were 'unlikely to provide much development

Table 1.6: Indicators of External Debt for Developing Economies, 1970–89 (%)

Economy/Groupings	*Total External Debt to GDP*			*Interest Payments to Exports*		
	1970–75	*1976–82*	*1983–89*	*1970–75*	*1976–82*	*1983–89*
Low-income	10.2	14.8	28.5	2.9	4.3	9.8
Low-income, excluding China and India	20.5	28.5	60.7	2.9	5.3	11.8
Middle-income	18.6	3.4.6	54.9	5.1	11	15.4
Argentina	20.1	46.1	80.3	14.1	17.9	41.6
Brazil	16.3	28.2	42	12.1	28.5	30.3
Morocco	18.6	55.1	109.5	2.8	13	17.1
Philippines	20.7	45.8	79.2	4.2	14.1	20.5

Source: World Bank (1991: Table 6.2).

finance in the years to come'. Further, bond markets would not be accessible for the heavily indebted countries. Therefore, private capital flows to the debtor countries had to focus on other forms, and FDI was the 'immediately obvious candidate' (ibid.).

Two financial arrangements for helping the indebted countries grow out of their indebtedness found more mention than the others: increased flows of FDI and debt-conversion (and especially debt-equity swap) mechanisms,[7] the latter being the indirect infusion of FDI into debt-stricken economies (ibid.: 1431). These two forms found favour especially because these were 'non-debt creating', an important consideration for the debt-burdened countries. Simultaneously, it was also argued that FDI was a 'safer form of finance' (Fernández-Arias and Hausmann 2001: 93) and that it was less volatile as compared to all other forms as also the 'most dependable source of foreign investment' (Lipsey 1999: 326).

While developing countries were keen to increase the inflows of FDI, the critical issue was the policy environment in the recipient countries that would induce favourable responses from the investors. The 1990s marked a watershed in this respect as almost all developing countries adopted foreign investor-friendly regimes.

FDI in the 1990s and After

The resurrection of FDI since the 1990s has been captured in a large body of literature produced since the early 1990s whose principal objective was to provide guidance to the developing countries for attracting larger inflows of FDI. The typical prescription for the recipient countries has been succinctly stated in Edwards (1990: 10): (a) reforming the foreign sector by opening up international trade; (b) reducing the size of government; (c) at least maintaining, but preferably increasing, their degree of international competitiveness; and (d) increasing the rate of domestic investment, which would then tend to see an increase in their level of direct foreign investment. Elements of this prescription were accepted as the norm by most developing countries.

The ideological underpinning of economic liberalisation was the Washington Consensus, a set of 10 prescriptions that were 'widely held in Washington' as necessary 'in most or all Latin American countries as of 1989' (Williamson 2004: 1475).[8] Included in this list of prescriptions were policies regarding the treatment of FDI. John Williamson, the principal architect of Washington Consensus, provided the rationale for opening the doors to FDI:

> a restrictive attitude limiting the entry of foreign direct investment (FDI) is regarded as foolish. Such investment can bring needed capital, skills, and know-how, either producing goods needed for the domestic market or contributing new exports. The main motivation for restricting FDI is economic nationalism, which Washington disapproves of, at least when practiced by countries other than the United States. (Williamson 1990)

Dani Rodrik provided a pointed criticism of the framework of the Washington Consensus. Rodrik's basic contention was that the framework of economic liberalisation included several elements that had to be rejected outright. As regards liberalisation of FDI, Rodrik (2002) argued that 'encouraging foreign investment or liberalizing everything and then waiting for things to happen will not work'. Rodrik was clearly proposing a more proactive policy regime that could secure tangible benefits from FDI.

In contrast to what Rodrik suggested, policy regimes for dealing with FDI evolved very differently in developing countries. Initially, the recipient countries 'liberalised their enabling frameworks for FDI' (Sauvant 2001: 40). This phenomenon was common right across the world. Data provided by United Nations Conference on

Trade and Development (UNCTAD) showed that in the year 2000, out of about 150 FDI regulatory changes made by 69 countries, 98 per cent were aimed at 'creating a more favourable environment for FDI' (ibid.). When such 'passive liberalisation' did not result in sufficient investment flows, governments turned to the second-generation policies to attract investment. These policies were adopted to 'actively market' their countries as locations for FDI.

The relationship between the FDI and their host countries went through several phases from the early post-World War II decades. In the 1950s and 1960s, the relationship between the host country and FDI was largely dependent on the policies adopted by the US. While in the earlier decade, the principal creditor nation promoted FDI, as its balance of payments situation deteriorated in the 1960s, the US resorted to coercive methods to regulate foreign investors. After being dominated by bank finance in the 1970s and 1980s, FDI has become one of the centrepieces of the policies of economic liberalisation since the 1990s. In Chapter 2, we shall provide the conceptual framework for understanding FDI.

Notes

1. In President Truman words, spoken at his inaugural address: 'Our aim should be to help the free peoples of the world, through their own efforts, to produce more food, more clothing, more materials for housing, and more mechanical power to lighten their burdens' (Truman 1949b).

2. The Gold Dollar Standard was the fixed exchange rate mechanism underlying the Bretton Woods system. This mechanism gave the US dollar the *de facto* position of an international reserve currency by making all currencies pegged to the US dollar. The value of the dollar was, in turn, determined by its parity to gold—one ounce of gold was equivalent to $35. Importantly, the US Federal Reserve had agreed to convert dollars at this gold parity rate.

3. The justification of our characterisation of governments as 'quasi regulators' will be provided in Chapter 4, where we discuss India's policies towards FDI.

4. According to Nurkse, foreign investments from private sources behaved differently from those from government or official sources, the difference being that private investors needed inducements before making their investments, while official investors did not require any such investments and were 'autonomous' (Kattel, Kriegal and Reinhart 2011: 82).

5. International Development Act of 1950.

6. The US signed the first Treaty of Friendship, Commerce and Navigation with Italy in early 1948, and later in the same year, a similar agreement was signed with Uruguay (Brown, Jr 1950: 486). These were the first evidences of international investment agreements, although the first formal agreement was formalised between West Germany and Pakistan in 1958.

7. Chandra (1988: 632) has argued that there was 'some evidence that in the recent past the debt-equity swaps have partly replaced the traditional mode of foreign investment'.

8. The term 'Washington Consensus' was coined by John Williamson in 1989 to describe a 10-point agenda for ushering in pro-market economic reforms (Williamson 2003: 1475; see also Williamson 2004).

References

Adler, Michael. 1971. 'The Impact of the U. S. Direct Investment Controls'. *Journal of International Business Studies* 2 (1): Spring: 1–14.

Brown, Jr, William Adams. 1950. 'Treaty, Guaranty, and Tax Inducements for Foreign Investments'. *American Economic Review* 40 (2), papers and proceedings of the sixty-second annual meeting of the American Economic Association, May: 486–94.

Cardoso, E., and R. Dornbusch. 1989. 'Foreign Private Capital Flows'. In *Handbook of Development Economics*, Volume 2, eds Hollis Chenery and T. N. Srinivasan, 1387–1441. Amsterdam: North Holland.

Chandra, Nirmal Kumar. 1988. 'Debt-Equity Swaps: New Way out of International Debt Crisis?'. *Economic and Political Weekly* 23 (13), 26 March: 631–32.

Dooley, Michael P. 1994. 'A Retrospective on the Debt Crisis'. Working paper no. 4963, National Bureau of Economic Research, Cambridge, December.

Dutt, Amitava Krishna. 1998. 'Direct Foreign Investment, Transnational Corporations and Growth: Some Empirical Evidence and a North-South Model'. In *Transnational Corporations and the Global Economy*, eds Richard Kozul-Wright and Robert Rawthorn, 164–91. London: Macmillan Press.

Edwards, Sebastian. 1990. 'Capital Flows, Foreign Direct Investment, and Debt-Equity Swaps in Developing Countries'. Working paper no. 3497, National Bureau of Economic Research, October. Available at http://www.nber.org/papers/w3497.pdf (accessed 15 March 2018).

Executive Order No. 11387, 33 Federal Register 47. 1968. Reproduced in 'United States: Mandatory Controls on Investment Abroad', *International Legal Materials* 7 (1), January: 53–86.

Feldstein, Martin (ed.). 1991. 'The Risk of Economic Crisis: Introduction'. In *The Risk of Economic Crisis*, 1–18. Chicago and London: University of Chicago Press.

Fernández-Arias, Eduardo and Ricardo Hausmann. 2001. 'Capital Inflows and Crisis: Does the Mix Matter?'. OECD Foreign Direct Investment Versus Other Flows to Latin America: Development Centre Seminars, Inter-American Development Bank and Development Centre of the Organisation for Economic Co-operation and Development, Paris.

Hunter, John M. 1953. 'Long-term Foreign Investment and Underdeveloped Countries'. *Journal of Political Economy* 61 (1): 15.

Joint Economic Committee. 1971. 'The Balance-of-Payments Mess: Hearings before the Subcommittee on International Exchange and Payments of the Joint Economic Committee'. Congress of the United States, 92nd Congress, first session, Washington, D. C. Available at https://www.jec.senate.gov/reports/92nd%20Congress/The%20Balance-of-Payments%20Mess%20(518).pdf (accessed 10 March 2018).

Kattel, Rainer, Jan A. Kregel and Erik S. Reinert. 2011. *Ragnar Nurkse: Trade and Development*. London: Anthem Press.

Lipsey, Robert E. 1999. 'The Role of Foreign Direct Investment in International Capital Flows'. In *International Capital Flows*, ed. Martin Feldstein, 307–31. Chicago: University of Chicago Press.

_____. 2001. 'Foreign Direct Investment and the Operations of Multinational Firms: Concepts, History, and Data'. Working paper no. 8665, National Bureau of Economic Research. Available at htp://www.nber.org/papers/w8665 (accessed 5 June 2018).

McGuire, Patrick and Nikola Tarashev. 2006. 'The International Banking Market'. *BIS Quarterly Review*, June. Available at https://www.bis.org/publ/qtrpdf/r_qt0606b.pdf (accessed 10 March 2018).

Meier, Gerald M. 1966. 'Legal-economic Problems of Private Foreign Investment in Developing Countries'. *University of Chicago Law Review* 33 (3), Spring: 463–93.

Nurkse, Ragnar. 2011. 'Problems of Capital Formation in Underdeveloped Countries'. In *Ragnar Nurkse: Trade and Development*, eds Rainer Kattel, Jan A. Kregel and Erik S. Reinert, 99–212. London: Anthem Press.

Penrose, Edith Tilton. 1956. 'Foreign Investment and the Growth of the Firm'. *Economic Journal* 66 (262), June: 220–35.

Rodrik, Dani. 2002. 'Abandon Neo-liberalism'. *Jakarta Post*, 1 October. Available at https://www.globalpolicy.org/global-taxes/44295.html (accessed 17 August 2018).

Sauvant, Karl. 2001. 'Recent FDI Trends, Implications for Developing Countries and Policy Challenges, in OECD'. New Horizons for Foreign Direct Investment, OECD Global Forum on International Investment, Paris.

Strauber, Rachel. 1970. 'Voluntary Foreign Credit Restraint and the Nonbank Financial Institutions'. *Financial Analysts Journal* 26 (3), May–June: 10–12, 87–89.

Triffin, Robert. 1966. 'The Balance of Payments and the Foreign Investment Position of the United States'. *Essays in International Finance* 55, International Finance Section, Department of Economics, Princeton University.

Truman, Harry S. 1949a. 'The President's Message to the Congress on "Point Four Legislation"'. *Annals of the American Academy of Political and Social Science* 268, March: 184–87.

_____. 1949b. 'Inaugural Address'. Harry S. Truman Presidential Library and Museum, 20 January. Available at https://www.trumanlibrary.org/whistlestop/50yr_archive/inagural20jan1949.htm (accessed 15 June 2018).

United Nations. 1951. 'Measures for the Economic Development of Under-developed Countries'. New York.

Willey, H. David. 1970. 'Direct Investment Controls and the Balance of Payments'. In *The International Corporation: A Symposium*, ed. Charles P. Kindleberger, 95–119. Cambridge, Massachusetts: MIT Press.

Williamson, John. 1990. 'What Washington Means by Policy Reform'. Peterson Institute for International Economics. Available at https://piie.com/commentary/speeches-papers/what-washington-means-policy-reform (accessed 20 June 2018).

_____. 2003. 'The Washington Consensus and Beyond'. *Economic and Political Weekly* 38 (15), 12–18 April: 1475–81.

_____. 2004. 'The Washington Consensus as Policy Prescription for Development'. Lecture in the series 'Practitioners of Development', delivered at the World Bank, 13 January. Available at https://piie.com/publications/papers/williamson0204.pdf (accessed 20 June 2018).

World Bank. 1981. 'World Development Report 1981'. World Bank, Washington, D. C. Available at https://openknowledge.worldbank.org/bitstream/handle/10986/5964/WDR%201981%20-%20English.pdf (accessed 20 July 2018).

World Bank. 1985. 'World Development Report 1985'. World Bank, Washington, D. C. Available at https://openknowledge.worldbank.org/bitstream/handle/10986/5968/WDR%201985%20-%20English.pdf (accessed 20 July 2018).

_____. 1991. 'World Development Report 1985'. World Bank, Washington, D. C. Available at https://openknowledge.worldbank.org/bitstream/handle/10986/5974/WDR%201991%20-%20English.pdf (accessed 20 July 2018).

two

Conceptualising FDI

Any discussion on foreign investment brings into focus the forms in which intra- and inter-corporate capital flows take place. Our objective in this chapter is, therefore, to discuss the key characteristics of FDI, one of the principal forms of capital flows between commercial enterprises. More specifically, we will explore the essential features of FDI and how this form of capital can be distinguished from some of the other forms of intra- and inter-enterprise capital flows, especially foreign portfolio investment (FPI).

Understanding the distinction between FDI and other forms of capital inflows, including FPI, is critical for two reasons. First, FDI provides not only investible funds to developing countries, but also technology and managerial expertise, which was described in Chapter 1 as the 'package of intangibles'. Over the past decades, research on FDI, which includes studies that have analysed the functioning of direct investment companies in their host countries, has seen a huge increase.[1] However, our assessment of a large cross-section of these studies is that most scholars have not considered the essential characteristics of FDI while studying this form of capital. In our view, this is a major lacuna, for, as we shall discuss in this chapter, it is important to understand how official agencies have conceptualised FDI before they capture and collate data. The impact of FDI on host economies critically hinges on the definition of FDI.

The second reason why understanding the distinction between FDI and other forms of capital inflows must be made is because governments of developing countries usually attach a premium to the former. While identifying financial resources for development, these governments have increasingly given a prominent place to FDI inflows. Moreover, it is common for governments to make efforts to attract such inflows by providing direct and indirect incentives to foreign companies.

The incentives that developing-country governments extend to FDI can take a number of forms; here, we will allude to three. First, these countries provide tax incentives to foreign companies that are common in construction, information technology (IT) and electronics, machinery and equipment, and other manufacturing sectors (Andersen, Kett and von Uexkull 2018: 75). Second, governments have continually expanded the scope of operation of foreign companies through deregulation and privatisation. The expansion of FDI inflows has often occurred at the expense of the domestic enterprises in recipient countries, largely the micro, small and medium enterprises (MSMEs). With governments increasingly tying the fortunes of their economic development programmes to FDI inflows, the cumulative impact of such inflows on the domestic enterprises has been far-reaching. One evidence of the adverse impact of FDI is the crowding-out of domestic investment (Dhar and Sinha Roy 1996).

A third set of incentives is provided through the BITs. Most developing countries have signed BITs for protecting and promoting foreign investments in their countries. Some studies have concluded that BITs have stimulated FDI flows into developing countries (Banga 2003: 34).[2]

Before we explore the reality behind the FDI numbers, let us focus on two related aspects of this form of capital. The first is the composition of FDI, and the second, and more important, is how FDI has been defined for the purposes of policymaking and presentation of data.

Composition of FDI

FDI usually has three components. The first is the inflow of equity capital from abroad, which adds to the country's capital stock, including plant and machinery, and is also called 'greenfield' investment. The second component is reinvested earnings of FDI enterprises, the undistributed profits of existing foreign enterprises in a country that are ploughed back. The third component is the acquisition of going enterprises by foreign investors, either through mergers or takeovers—the so-called 'brownfield' investments. As is obvious, the last form of FDI does not add to productive capacities in the host countries.

Fresh Infusion of Capital

For the host countries, 'greenfield' investments are the most preferred form of FDI, for they make net additions to the productive capacities. They also come with the maximum possibility of the host countries benefiting from the positive externalities in the form of intangibles like technology (know-how) and managerial skills provided by direct investors.

Retained Earnings

In its Benchmark Definition of Foreign Direct Investment (henceforth, 'Benchmark Definition'), the Organisation for Economic Cooperation and Development (OECD) defines retained earnings as the net current earnings of an FDI enterprise 'that are not distributed as dividends to the shareholders ... are deemed distributed, as investment income, to the direct investor ... proportionate to its holdings of shares'[3] in the enterprise (OECD 2008: 180). The UN System of National Accounts (SNA) explains that retained earnings of an FDI enterprise are to be treated as if they have been 'distributed and remitted to foreign direct investors in proportion to their ownership of the equity of the enterprise and then reinvested by them by means of additions to equity' (Commission of the European Communities et al. 1993: paragraph 7.120). The rationale behind this treatment of retained earnings is that since direct investment enterprises are under direct control, or influence, of foreign investors, the decision to retain some of the earnings of such enterprises 'must represent a deliberate investment decision' on the part of foreign direct investors. Retained earnings remain as reserves until they are converted into equity through issue of bonus shares.[4]

Mergers and Acquisitions

Mergers take place when two or more companies agree to combine into a single entity. Acquisitions, on the other hand, occur when the equity capital of one company or group of companies is bought by another company or group of companies. Although the two phenomena are different in their motivations, they are considered together, as they entail the taking over of existing entities, locally or foreign owned, by a foreign investor. Entities resulting from mergers or acquisitions (M&A) involving a foreign investor are identified as FDI enterprises.[5]

However, the Balance of Payments Manual (BPM) of the IMF does not consider M&A as separate items within direct investment. The BPM considers M&As differently from other forms of direct investments, as 'they may not provide any new financing for the firms involved but rather represent a change in investors' (IMF 2009: 135).

Data on M&As is provided by UNCTAD (2017a: 86) in its annual World Investment Reports. The cases included are of those merged or acquired enterprises that meet the criteria of FDI enterprises.

Identification of FDI: The Policy Discourse

What constitutes FDI has been extensively discussed by academics and policymakers for nearly a century. The beginnings of this tradition can be traced back to the first official survey of outward direct investment conducted by the US Department of Commerce for 1929. The survey was mandated to measure '... the amount of capital involved in the extension of American enterprise into foreign countries ...' (Lipsey 2001: 3). It made an analytically significant contribution to our understanding of FDI, for it made the all-important distinction between FDI and FPI.[6] FDI, according to the survey, included 'commercial and industrial properties situated abroad and belonging to residents of the US and its Territories, from which a return is normally expected'. It was defined as 'pure "interest" capital' invested in 'American-controlled corporations operating abroad' (ibid.: 4). FPI, on the other hand, was 'acquired through the purchase of foreign securities publicly offered and through the international securities movement', and was included as 'a part of the holding of American commercial and industrial corporations' (ibid.). In other words, in an FPI enterprise, a foreign investor did not hold the controlling stock.

Further clarity on 'control' as the distinguishing feature of FDI came in the next survey conducted in 1936. FDI enterprises were identified as those that were 'controlled by a person or small group of persons (corporate or natural) domiciled in the US, or in which such person or group has an important voice'. The factor of control was 'purposely emphasized in the definition, since it [was] considered to be the most significant basis for classifying investments' (ibid.). However, the survey did not provide a quantitative basis for assessing 'control'.

The quantitative basis of 'foreign control' for the purposes of identifying FDI, was provided for the first time in 1941 when US Treasury conducted a Census of Foreign Owned Assets in the country, including that of 'foreign controlled United States enterprises'. This census determined 'foreign control' based on ownership of 25 per cent or more of the voting stock by foreigners (Wilkins 1999: 72).

The US Department of Commerce conducted the outward investment survey for 1950 which provided a somewhat detailed categorisation of investments abroad, including those that were substantially controlled by US investors. Four categories of FDI were identified in the survey. These were:

1. foreign corporations, whose voting securities amounting to 25 per cent or more were owned by persons or groups of affiliated persons, ordinarily US residents;
2. foreign corporations, whose voting stock in the aggregate amounting to 50 per cent or more was publicly held within the US, but distributed among stockholders, so that no investor, or group of affiliated investors, owned less than 25 per cent;
3. sole proprietorships, partnerships or real property (other than property held for the personal use of the owner) held abroad by residents of the US; and
4. foreign branches of US corporations (Lipsey 2001: 5).

In the subsequent decades, the threshold of foreign ownership for determining 'control' by foreigners was lowered. The US Department of Commerce lowered the threshold to 10 per cent in the 1960s. This was done first for US businesses abroad and, subsequently, for foreign businesses in the US (Wilkins 1999: 72).

The Foreign Direct Investment Regulations introduced by President Lyndon B. Johnson in 1968 provided one of the early evidences that the US administration had diluted the ownership criteria. We discussed in Chapter 1 that the Regulations were aimed at preventing American companies from investing abroad, given the country's deteriorating balance of payments situation.

The Regulations defined 'direct investor' in the context of outward flows of FDI from the US as

> ... any person within the US who directly or indirectly owned or acquired:
> (a) 10% or more of the total combined voting power of any foreign national; or
> (b) The right or power to receive, control, or otherwise enjoy 10% or more of the earnings, receipts, income or profits of any foreign national;
> (c) The right or power to receive, control or otherwise direct the disposition of 10% or more of the assets of any foreign national upon the liquidation. (*International Legal Materials* 1968: 56)

The International Investment Survey Act of 1976 provided the conclusive evidence that the US had adopted the criterion of 10 per cent of voting share for identifying direct investment (henceforth, the '10 per cent rule').[7]

The International Practice

The IMF tried to follow the developments in the largest creditor nation for benchmarking FDI, which it needed to provide guidance to its member states regarding their balance of payments. The first of such guidance appeared in the third edition of its Balance of Payments Manual in 1961 (BPM3). IMF defined 'direct investment' as an investment 'made to create some kind of permanent interest in an enterprise' (IMF 1961: paragraph 367). Since it was intended to create or expand a permanent interest in business, direct investment, according to IMF, was not likely to be reversed and was unlikely to vary in the short run, as was the case with most other forms of investment (ibid.: paragraph 369).

The threshold of foreign ownership that IMF proposed for identifying control was similar to that adopted by the US legal system, namely 25 per cent of the voting stock by a closely organised group of non-residents (ibid.: paragraph 373).

The IMF revised its Balance of Payments Manual in 1977 (BPM4), and its characterisation of 'direct investment' underwent changes. The two features of FDI identified in BPM3—the intrinsic link between ownership and control in a direct investment enterprise, and the long-term nature of the investment—were kept unchanged. Changes were, however, introduced in the threshold of voting share required to be held by the foreign direct investor for the investment to be counted as FDI. While so doing, BPM4 adopted an imprecise definition of FDI, stating that when foreign ownership was 'concentrated in the hands of one investor or a group of associates, the percentage chosen as providing evidence of direct investment ... frequently ranged from 25 per cent down to 10 per cent' (IMF 1977: paragraph 412).

By the early 1990s, a broad consensus had emerged between at least three policy-coordination agencies on the definition of FDI—the IMF, OECD and UN SNA. IMF pushed for a standardised definition of FDI so that a consistent framework for reporting the balance of payments position of its member countries could be developed. The UN, too, had a similar reporting function, in the national accounts of the member states. OECD's interest in a standardised definition was two-fold: one, develop a consistent reporting framework for its member states, and two, develop policy guidelines on monitoring foreign investment.

The efforts made by the IMF, OECD and UN to arrive at a consensus on the definition of FDI were reflected, respectively, in the approaches suggested in the IMF's Balance of Payments Manual (BPM5) adopted in 1993 (IMF 1993), the third edition of the OECD's Benchmark Definition of 1996 (OECD 1996) and the SNA of 1993 prepared by the Inter-secretariat Working Group on National Accounts under the aegis of the UN (Commission of the European Communities et al. 1993). In fact, the Inter-secretariat Working Group had the participation of the first two organisations, besides the European Commission and the World Bank. We will now discuss the manner in which FDI was conceptualised by the IMF and the OECD; the SNA incorporated the definitions given in BPM5 and the Benchmark Definition.

BPM5 defined direct investment as

> the category of international investment that reflects the objective of a resident entity in one economy obtaining a lasting interest in an enterprise resident in another economy ... The lasting interest implies the existence of a long-term relationship between the direct investor and the enterprise and a significant degree of influence by the investor on the management of the enterprise. Direct investment comprises not only the initial transaction establishing the relationship between the investor and the enterprise but also all subsequent transactions between them and among affiliated enterprises, both incorporated and unincorporated. (IMF 1993: paragraph 359)

A second element was included to identify a direct investment enterprise, which was based on the extent of ownership by a foreign investor. This was a departure from the definition of

FDI provided in BPM4, which, as mentioned earlier, was rather imprecise. BPM5 provided a more precise definition of a direct investment enterprise:[8] 'an incorporated or unincorporated enterprise in which a direct investor, who is resident in another economy, owns 10% or more of the ordinary shares or voting power (for an incorporated enterprise) or the equivalent (for an unincorporated enterprise)' (ibid.: paragraph 362).

Although BPM5 proposed the '10 per cent rule' for identifying direct investment, IMF members could also use twin parameters of ownership and control to identify FDI under the following circumstances: (a) in case the direct investor owned less than 10 per cent (or even none) of the ordinary shares of an enterprise but it had effective voice in management, this enterprise could be included as a direct investment enterprise; and (b) when the investor owned 10 per cent or more but did not have effective voice in management, the enterprise could be excluded.

According to OECD's Benchmark Definition, direct investment served the

> objective of obtaining a lasting interest by a resident entity in one economy ("direct investor") in an entity resident in an economy other than that of the investor ("direct investment enterprise"). The term "lasting interest" implied the existence of a long-term relationship between the direct investor and the enterprise and a significant degree of influence on the management. (OECD 1996: paragraph 5)

Endorsing the 10 per cent rule for determining the existence of a direct investment relationship, OECD clarified that an 'effective voice in the management, as evidenced by an ownership of at least 10 per cent, implies that the direct investor is able to influence or participate in the management of an enterprise; it does not require absolute control by the foreign investor' (ibid.: paragraph 8).

OECD also recognised that countries may not apply the 10 per cent rule for identifying FDI, since an investor may not be able to exercise any significant influence on an enterprise even while owning 10 per cent of the voting shares, while another may have an effective voice in management even with less than 10 per cent ownership. Under such circumstances, countries not following the 10 per cent rule were advised by the OECD to 'identify, where possible, the aggregate value of transactions not falling under the 10 per cent cut-off rule, so as to facilitate international comparability' (ibid.: paragraph 9).

The OECD also recognised that countries may consider the existence of elements of a direct investment relationship through a combination of factors listed in Box 2.1. The purpose behind OECD's enumeration of the possible factors for determining the existence or otherwise of a direct-investment relationship seems to be an attempt by the organisation to ensure transparency in the reporting of FDI, and that countries produce comparable sets of data.

Box 2.1: Elements of a Direct Investment Relationship (May Be Used Also in Combination)

1. Representation on the board of directors;
2. Participation in policymaking processes;
3. Material inter-company transactions;
4. Interchange of managerial personnel;
5. Provision of technical information;
6. Provision of long-term loans at lower than existing market rates.

Source: OECD (1996: 8).

The two main organisations involved in setting global benchmarks for identifying FDI revised their conceptual frameworks yet again in 2008. The IMF, in its sixth edition of the Balance of Payments Manual (BPM6), defined direct investment as a 'category of cross-border investment associated with a resident in one economy having control or a significant degree of influence on the management of an enterprise that is resident in another economy' (IMF 2009: paragraph 6.8). BPM6 added that since there is control or a significant degree of influence by the investor, 'direct investment tends to have different motivations and to behave in different ways from other forms of investment' (ibid.: paragraph 6.10).

One of the major changes introduced by BPM6 was the adoption of two separate yardsticks for 'control' and 'significant degree influence' of an FDI enterprise by the foreign investor. It may be recalled that these two yardsticks were earlier used interchangeably in the definition of 'direct investment'. In the revised framework, 'control' was determined to exist if the direct investor owned more than 50 per cent of the voting rights in an enterprise, while 'significant degree of influence' existed if the direct investor owned between 10 and 50 per cent of the voting rights.

The OECD, too, modified its definition of FDI in its fourth edition of the Benchmark Definition. FDI, according to this definition, was the form of investment used by the direct investor to establish 'a lasting interest' in an enterprise. 'Long-term relationship between the direct investor and the direct investment enterprise and a significant degree of influence on the management of the enterprise' (OECD 2008: paragraph 117), together with the 10 per cent rule, were indicators of 'lasting interest'. Thus, the OECD, too, adopted the criteria 'significant degree of influence' to describe the relationship of the foreign investor with an FDI enterprise, dispensing with 'control' as the criteria. Further, the past practice wherein OECD allowed the use of other elements mentioned in Box 2.1 for identifying FDI was discontinued; the new approach did 'not recommend the use of other considerations', which actually manifest control/influence (ibid.).

But while the IMF and OECD had diluted the criteria of ownership and control, the specialised body of the UN that is mandated to monitor foreign investment, UNCTAD (2017b: 3), followed the past practice of identifying FDI using the three-fold criteria, namely the '10 per cent rule', 'control' and 'substantial degree of influence' of the direct investor over the invested enterprise.

Over the past decades, the definition of FDI has undergone several significant changes. While in the earlier decades, ownership by the foreign investor above a threshold was used as the major criteria for identifying FDI, in the more recent decades, this criterion has been progressively diluted. Ownership by a foreign investor above the threshold meant that the investor exercised both 'control' and 'substantial degree of influence', and it was, therefore, a well-accepted proposition that the foreign investor would guide the fortunes of the invested enterprise. Further, the criteria mentioned earlier, put together, also implied that the foreign investor would have a lasting interest in the host country, and would, therefore, participate in the latter's development endeavours.

In Chapter 1, we discussed the dilution of the role of FDI as a source of long-term finance, and in this chapter, we saw a confirmation of this fact. The foreign ownership criteria necessary for identifying a company as FDI was diluted to 10 per cent from the earlier 25 per cent. Given that many of these companies were public limited and most were also widely held, a lower foreign shareholding was deemed sufficient for the foreign investor to exercise both control and substantial degree of influence over an enterprise. As long as the foreign investor had significant influence or control, the long-term stakes of the investor could also be guaranteed.

With the change in the definition of FDI towards the later part of the 2000s, the relationship between ownership on the one hand, and control and substantial degree of influence on the other, has become quite tenuous. The implications of adopting this framework for the host countries, in terms of the quality of FDI they have received in the recent past, are analysed in the following section by looking at the numbers from India.

Several generations of commentators have commented on the changing character of FDI, and their views for a complete understanding of the phenomenon are critical, in our view. A brief account of the perspective of the commentators is also presented in the following section.

The Indian Practice

India never provided a formal definition of a foreign-controlled company. In the decade of the 1960s and 1970s, regulations were adopted to limit foreign shareholding in companies, most significantly, through the Foreign Exchange Regulation Act (FERA) of 1973. But FERA, as we shall discuss in Chapter 4, was not intended to restrict foreign control over enterprises; as its title suggested, the Act provided mechanisms for limiting outgo of foreign exchange from the country.

The Reserve Bank of India (RBI) took up the task of identifying foreign-controlled companies for reporting on the country's foreign liabilities and assets. This exercise was taken up immediately after Independence in pursuance of the request of the IMF. In its Census of India's Foreign Liabilities and Assets (CIFLA), the RBI (1950) examined various concepts and definitions for CIFLA. The RBI concluded that a company could be treated as a foreign-controlled company if (a) 40 per cent or more of its shares were owned in any one country outside India, (b) it was a subsidiary of a parent company registered in any country abroad, (c) 25 per cent or more of its shares were owned by a foreign-controlled Indian joint stock company, which was not a managing agent, and (d) it was a company managed by a foreign-controlled managing agency company (ibid.: 36). The exercise was repeated by the RBI in the same format up to 1961, after which it has been publishing an annual survey of 'India's International Investment Position' of the (a) branches, (b) subsidiaries of foreign companies and (c) a select number of other undertakings having foreign equity capital. For purposes of the annual surveys, the RBI takes 25 per cent or more foreign equity in a company as a basis for classifying the company as under 'foreign control'.[9]

With India integrating increasingly with the global processes since the 1990s, efforts have been made to align the country's FDI reporting system with the international reporting system. This process was taken further following the recommendations of the Committee on Compilation of Foreign Direct Investment in India in 2002 (Government of India 2002). The Committee, even while recognising the fact that the benefits derived by direct investors go far beyond the investment income and that the investees often happen to be units of multinational operations, recommended that the way FDI was defined should 'facilitate external account recording'. It underlined that '... the concepts, definitions and classifications used [should be] internally consistent and support comparability of these statistics with other compilers. Secondly, the compilation of FDI statistics has to be based on internationally accepted BPM5' (ibid.: 10). The Committee's recommendations thus endorsed the criterion of 10 per cent voting power included in BPM5, and its further focus was essentially on the items to be included and procedures for collecting the information.

The upshot of this exercise was that the 10 per cent criterion was taken as the inviolable yardstick for determination of foreign influence over an enterprise, and all other aspects of FDI were ignored. In particular, the representative character of company-finance studies based on the new criteria compared to those based on foreign-controlled rupee companies (FCRCs) to reliably reflect the operations of FDI in India were also not discussed.

It needs to be spelt out that while India started reporting FDI inflows as per international best practices beginning 2000–01, following the recommendations of the Committee, the adoption of best practices has been confined to reporting reinvested earnings, equity capital of unincorporated foreign bodies and other associated capital (mainly loans). Besides meeting the international requirements, the unstated objective was also to make India's inflows look relatively healthy in comparison to those of China. Instead of applying the 10 per cent rule, however, all investments by persons/entities residing outside India in the capital of Indian companies other than those through the portfolio investment scheme were treated as FDI. RBI (2010) explains that

> while as per the international definition, for an investment to qualify as FDI the foreign investor needs to have a 10 per cent or higher stake in a given company, in India this has not been strictly adhered to. Irrespective of the extent of holding in a particular company, it is considered as an FDI if the non-resident acquires shares in a company other than by way of acquisition from the stock market, i.e., through initial public offerings (IPO) or through private arrangements ... (Ibid.: 82)

Thus, credit (inflows) under FDI 'to India' includes all types of investments in equities (investments made by non-residents in the shares/mandatorily-convertible debentures/preference shares of an Indian company), reinvested earnings of both incorporated and unincorporated bodies (mainly foreign bank branches operating in India) and other capital of FDI companies. 'Other' under FDI includes inter-corporate loans given by parent companies (group) to their affiliates.

The fact of non-adherence to the 10 per cent criterion, ignoring the context surrounding FDI, was found to be problematic in many quarters. Significantly, the Economic Advisory Council to the Prime Minister in its Review of the Economy 2007–08 said:

> Inflows of Private Equity (PE) investments have also been quite large. Since in most cases PE flows constitute less than 10% of the capital of the company being invested they should ideally be reported under Portfolio Capital, and not under FDI. *It is not clear what the current accounting practice is* (emphasis added). (Economic Advisory Council to the Prime Minister 2008: 25)

What gets clearly reflected in this statement is the fact that an important official advisory body was unaware of certain aspects of computing FDI in India.

The thin line between FDI and FPI, as far as classification of foreign private equity and venture capital in India are concerned, is further evident from the following observation of the Working Group on Foreign Investment set up by the Ministry of Finance.

> Inflows into unlisted equity: At a conceptual level, a private equity or venture capital fund outside India can invest in India in three ways. First, private investment in unlisted equity can take place if the foreign entity creates an investment vehicle which obtains an FII [foreign institutional investment] registration. Second, even without registering as an FII a private equity or venture capital fund outside India can invest in an Indian unlisted company up to the level of caps for FIIs. These investments would be treated as FDI ... These two mechanisms, put together, characterize the main avenues for private equity/venture capital inflows into India. The third way for private equity or venture capital funds outside India to invest in the country is to register as an FVCI [foreign venture capital investor] with SEBI [Securities and Exchange Board of India] and be regulated as such. (RBI 2010: 71)

The Consolidated FDI Policy (CFP) issued on 31 March 2010 by then Department of Industrial Policy and Promotion (DIPP), renamed the Department for Promotion of Industry and Internal

Trade (DPIIT), and its predecessor, Draft Press Note (DPN) on the FDI Regulatory Framework, throw light on the way FDI is being measured in India. While reiterating the motivation of the direct investor as '... a strategic long term relationship with the direct investment enterprise to ensure the significant degree of influence by the direct investor in the management of the direct investment enterprise' (Government of India 2010: 5), the CFP further explained: 'Investment in Indian companies can be made both by non-resident as well as resident Indian entities. *Any non-resident investment in an Indian company is direct foreign investment*' (emphasis added) (ibid.: 24).

Interestingly, the DPN issued earlier for discussion by the government stated that: 'In India the "lasting interest" is not evinced by any minimum holding of percentage of equity capital/shares/voting rights in the investment enterprise' (ibid.: 1).

This suggests that all foreign investments (other than those purchased by FIIs on the stock market) in equity capital and equity-related instruments are being treated as FDI, irrespective of the extent of foreign share. It is obvious that there will not be lasting interest and the ability or intention to significantly influence the management of the investee company in all the cases. While this contrasts sharply with the 'international best practice', one cannot expect such FDI to be accompanied by the attendant attributes and deliver the perceived benefits from FDI.

Conceptualisation of FDI in Available Literature

Commentators in the early post-World War II period identified FDI using the yardstick of the foreign investors' 'control' over the functioning of the invested enterprise, even though the degree of control exercised was a more difficult distinction to apply

(Hunter 1953: 16). The earlier studies differentiated between FDI and FPI based on whether the foreign investor had substantial control over an enterprise to be able to direct its activities and, therefore, anticipate returns from the investment (ibid.). Another characterisation of FDI was that this component of foreign capital flows brought with it 'significant element of ownership, control, and management' over an enterprise; in other words, they were 'entrepreneurial investments' (Maffry 1954: 614). According to Penrose (1956),

> in the realm of manufacturing this kind of investment is probably more effective in expanding productivity and promoting industrial efficiency than any other kind of foreign investment. Its advantages derive largely from the fact that behind the new foreign firm are the resources and experience of the parent concern, including not only managerial and technical personnel but also that indefinable advantage in its internal operations which an efficient going concern usually has over a new one. (Ibid.: 225)

Penrose also pointed out that FDI multiplied itself by ploughing back the earnings of the enterprises that received such inflows.[10] Thus, commentators not only endorsed the definition adopted by policymakers, but added an important factor, namely the long-term association with the host country, as yet another key characteristic of FDI.

More recent literature has dwelled on the nature of FDI in somewhat greater detail. Wilkins (1999) points out that a foreign direct investor invests abroad as part of a business strategy with a view to exercising ownership and control, potential for control, or at least influence. Such an investor 'intends to be "active" ... whereby it plans to obtain a return based not only on its financial contribution, but also on its transfer of intangible assets, its way of doing business and its technology (broadly construed)' (ibid.: 56). This feature of FDI takes us back once again to Chapter 1, where we argued that this form of investment is understood not only as a form of capital flow, but also as a package, combining capital and the critical intangibles for an enterprise, namely technology and managerial expertise.

While studies on FDI have proliferated over time, only a small proportion of them have made serious efforts to not only lay bare the features of this form of capital flow, but perhaps, more importantly, attempt to make a distinction between FDI and the various other forms of capital flow, including FPI. Commentators who have dwelled on these have made the distinction between the forms of foreign capital flows by tracing them back to their historical patterns.

Most studies argue that the period before 1914 was dominated by FPI. Dunning (1970) estimates that in 1914, 90 per cent of all international capital flows were FPI. Included in such capital flows were acquisition of securities issued by foreign institutions, without any control over, or participation in the management of, the entities concerned. Dunning also pointed out that although several American and European companies had owned sizeable foreign manufacturing ventures, these involvements 'were the exceptions rather than the rule'; they 'rarely accounted for a major part of the enterprises' total activities' (ibid.: 2). This was hardly surprising given that the corporations, which, in the later decades, were the main drivers of FDI flows, began consolidating their position in the global economy only after the World War I.

Lipsey (1999: 10) suggests that FDI and FPI can be 'thought of as ways of dividing up risks among different types of investors and borrowers'. In the early history of the US, for instance, early foreign investment went mainly into government securities, considered relatively safe. Later foreign investors focused on investments into railroads. Lipsey explains that 'foreign portfolio investment went to large, lumpy, social overhead capital projects, railroads, canals, and later, public utilities, relatively safer investments and less dependent on local knowledge than the typically much smaller, and on that account, riskier enterprises in agriculture or manufacturing, which were left mainly to local financing' (ibid.: 313).

Based on the patterns of participation of FDI and FPI in foreign enterprises, Wilkins (1999) provides an important analytical construct. The author makes four distinctions between FDI and FPI, drawing on Dunning and Dilyard (1999): (a) FDI includes the transfer of non-financial, as well as financial assets; (b) FDI involves continuing control, while FPI does not; (c) FDI is usually more lumpy and indivisible than FPI; and (d) FPI tends to be prompted by financial returns that are higher abroad than those at home, while motivations for individual FDI projects are far broader (Wilkins 1999: 57–58). The last-mentioned distinction holds the key, for it enumerates the essential character of FDI as a critical input in the development model adopted, especially by the developing countries in recent decades.

Several studies have commented on the dilution in the criteria for identifying FDI and the consequent implications for identifying FDI enterprises. According to Lipsey (1999):

> [O]ver time, the definition of direct investment has shifted from an emphasis on control across national boundaries to a vaguer notion of "lasting interest" and a "significant" influence on management, and in the balance of payments data the enterprise is divided up statistically among owners of shares of 10 per cent or more. (Ibid.: 23)

This situation is well summarised by Soci (2007: 227): the idea of 'control', which was present in earlier definitions, has been abandoned in favour of a broader though no less vague concept. What 'lasting interest' means is

> a stake of 10% or more of the ordinary shares or voting power of an incorporated enterprise or the equivalent of an unincorporated

> enterprise ... This is the threshold in the US, whereas the legislation in the European Union is not yet completely uniform. The immediate consequence of an FDI is that a national firm acting as above becomes, by definition, a multinational enterprise. (Ibid.)

Table 2.1 summarises some of these conceptual distinctions between FDI and FPI.

Table 2.1: Conceptually Segregating FDI and FPI

FDI	*FPI*
Greenfield	Greenfield
M&A	M&A
Control	Some possibility of control
Long term	Not long term
Technology	Little scope
Management	Some possibility
Brand names	No
Trade with related parties	No

Source: Compiled by the authors.

Notes

1. The earlier studies were captured in two exceptional surveys by Cardoso and Dornbusch (1989) and Helleiner (1989).

2. An UNCTAD (2014) survey of the studies on BITs also showed that these treaties have had a positive impact on FDI. However, a more recent survey conducted by the Bonnitcha (2017: 4) concludes that 'investment treaties are more effective in attracting the types of FDI that are less beneficial from a host country perspective'.

3. OECD (2008) explains that it is the direct investor's 'percentage holding of shares on issue (or equivalent) that determines the ratio under which reinvested earnings are deemed distributed, not the level of voting power'.

4. Helleiner (1989) provides a neat analytical explanation of the inclusion of retained earnings as FDI:

> ... when retained earnings are employed for the financing of investment they should be thought of analytically as constituting an external payment (foreign earnings) followed by an external inflow of investment. If such investments are freely made they are obviously just as important as any "fresh" capital inflow; earnings on previous foreign investment are as surely foreign as are those from any other payment for an import. If external payments are controlled, as they frequently are, foreign firms may have few options but reinvestment in their own activities (which are usually more attractive than, say, government bonds or bank deposits). (Ibid.: 1455)

5. See the discussion on identification of FDI later in this chapter.

6. However, Wilkins (2004: 70), through her extensive research on foreign investment in the US, has shown that there can be 'conceptual difficulties in distinguishing FDI and FPI'.

7. The Act used the following language to define direct investment: 'ownership or control, directly or indirectly, by one person of 10 per centum or more of voting securities or an incorporated business enterprise or an equivalent interest in an unincorporated enterprise' [International Investment Survey Act 1976, Public Law 94–472, Section 3(10)].

8. BPM5 provides a more elaborate definition of direct investment enterprises: 'those entities that are subsidiaries (a non-resident investor owns more than 50 percent), associates (an investor owns 50 percent or less) and branches (wholly or jointly owned unincorporated enterprises) either directly or indirectly owned by the direct investor' (IMF 1993: paragraph 362).

9. The RBI adopted this definition after 1970–71. By way of a footnote to the survey, the RBI introduced the new definition which has been followed ever since. See RBI (1973).

10. 'Direct foreign investment – and by this I mean the ownership and operation of business organisations in a foreign country' (Penrose 1956: 220).

References

'International Investment Survey Act of 1976'. 1976. Public Law 94–472, 11 October.

Executive Order No. 11387, 33 Federal Register 47. 1968. Reproduced in 'United States: Mandatory Controls on Investment Abroad', *International Legal Materials* 7 (1), January: 53–86.

Andersen, Maria R., Benjamin R. Kett and Erik von Uexkull. 2018. 'Corporate Tax Incentives and FDI in Developing Countries'. In *Global Investment Competitiveness Report 2017/2018: Foreign Investor Perspectives and Policy Implications*, 73–99. Washington, D. C.: World Bank.

Banga, Rashmi. 2003. 'Impact of Government Policies and Investment Agreements on FDI Inflows'. Working paper no. 116, Indian Council for Research on International Economic Relations, New Delhi. Available at http://icrier.org/pdf/WP116.pdf (accessed 15 July 2018).

Bonnitcha, Jonathan. 2017. 'Assessing the Impacts of Investment Treaties: Overview of the Evidence'. International Institute for Sustainable Development, Manitoba, Canada. Available at https://www.iisd.org/sites/default/files/publications/assessing-impacts-investment-treaties.pdf (accessed 10 July 2018).

Cardoso, E., and R. Dornbusch. 1989. 'Foreign Private Capital Flows'. In *Handbook of Development Economics*, Volume 2, eds Hollis Chenery and T. N. Srinivasan, 1387–1441. Amsterdam: North Holland.

Commission of the European Communities, IMF, OECD, United Nations and World Bank. 1993. *System of National Accounts*. Prepared under the auspices of the Inter-Secretariat Working Group on National Accounts, United Nations, Brussels/Luxembourg, New York, Paris and Washington, D. C.

Dhar, Biswajit and Saikat Sinha Roy. 1996. 'Foreign Direct Investment and Domestic Savings-Investment Behaviour: Developing Countries' Experience'. *Economic and Political Weekly* 31 (35–37), special number, September: 2547–51.

Dunning, John. 1970. *Studies in International Investment*. London: George Allen and Unwin.

Dunning, John and John Dilyard. 1999. 'Towards a General Paradigm of Foreign Direct and Foreign Portfolio Investment'. *Transnational Corporations* 8 (1), April: 1–52.

Economic Advisory Council to the Prime Minister. 2008. 'Review of the Economy 2007/08'. New Delhi. Available at http://eac.gov.in/reports/rev_eco0708.pdf (accessed 25 July 2018).

Government of India. 2002. 'Committee on Compilation of Foreign Direct Investment in India'. Department of Industrial Policy and Promotion, October. Available at http://dipp.nic.in/sites/default/files/fdi.pdf (accessed 25 July 2018).

______. 2010. 'Draft Press Note No. (2010): FDI Regulatory Framework'. Department of Industrial Policy and Promotion, Ministry of Commerce and Industry. Available at http://dipp.nic.in/sites/default/files/pn9_2009_1.pdf (accessed 25 July 2018).

Helleiner, G. K. 1989. 'Transnational Corporations and Direct Foreign Investment'. In *Handbook of Development Economics*, Volume 2, eds H. Chenery and T. N. Srinivasan, 1441–80. Amsterdam: North Holland.

Hunter, John M. 1953. 'Long-term Foreign Investment and Underdeveloped Countries'. *Journal of Political Economy* 61 (1): 15.

IMF. 1961. 'Balance of Payments Manual', third edition. Washington, D. C.

______. 1977. 'Balance of Payments Manual', fourth edition. Washington, D. C.

______. 1993. 'Balance of Payments Manual', fifth edition. Washington, D. C.

______. 2009. 'Balance of Payments and International Investment Position Manual', sixth edition. Washington, D. C.

Lipsey, Robert E. 1999. 'The Role of Foreign Direct Investment in International Capital Flows'. In *International Capital Flows*, ed. Martin Feldstein, 307–31. Chicago: University of Chicago Press.

______. 2001. 'Foreign Direct Investment and the Operations of Multinational Firms: Concepts, History, and Data'. Working paper no. 8665, National Bureau of Economic Research. Available at htp://www.nber.org/papers/w8665 (accessed 5 June 2018).

Maffry, August. 1954. 'Direct Versus Portfolio Investment in the Balance of Payments'. *American Economic Review* 44 (2), papers and proceedings of the 66th annual meeting of the American Economic Association, May: 614–623.

OECD. 1996. 'OECD Benchmark Definition of Foreign Direct Investment', third edition. Paris.

______. 2008. 'OECD Benchmark Definition of Foreign Direct Investment', fourth edition. Paris.

Penrose, Edith Tilton. 1956. 'Foreign Investment and the Growth of the Firm'. *Economic Journal* 66 (262), June: 220–35.

RBI. 1950. 'Report on the Census of India's Foreign Liabilities and Assets as on 30th June 1948'. Examiner Press, Bombay.

______. 1973. 'Finances of Branches of Foreign Companies and Foreign Controlled Rupee Companies'. *Reserve Bank of India Bulletin*, October.

______. 2010. 'Report of the Working Group on Balance of Payments Manual for India'. September. Available at https://www.rbi.org.in/scripts/PublicationReportDetails.aspx?UrlPage=&ID=596 (accessed 10 July 2018).

Soci, Ann. 2007. 'FDI: A Difficult Connection between Theory and Empirics'. In *New Directions in Economic Geography*, ed. Bernard Fingleton, 277–314. Cheltenham, UK: Edward Elgar.

UNCTAD. 2014. 'The Impact of International Investment Agreements on Foreign Direct Investment: An Overview of Empirical Studies 1998–2014, IIA Issues Note'. September. Available at http://investmentpolicyhub.unctad.org/Upload/Documents/unctad-web-diae-pcb-2014-Sep%2024.pdf (accessed 15 June 2018).

______. 2017a. 'World Investment Report 2017: Investment and the Digital Economy'. Geneva.

______. 2017b. 'Methodological Note, World Investment Report 2017: Investment and the Digital Economy'. Geneva.

Wilkins, Mira. 1999. 'Two Literatures, Two Story-lines: Is a General Paradigm of Foreign Portfolio and Foreign Direct Investment Feasible?'. *Transnational Corporations* 8 (1), April: 53–116.

______. 2004. *The History of Foreign Investment in the United States, 1914–1945*. Cambridge, Massachusetts and London, England: Harvard University Press.

three

Trends in Global FDI Flows

In this chapter, we will discuss the trends in global FDI flows since 1970. The choice of the initial year is dictated by the availability of data, which we shall collate from two sources. The first source is the IMF and the second is UNCTAD. It may be recalled that in Chapter 2, we had relied on these two sources for functional definitions of FDI. In the following sections, we will put the numbers to the categories that we borrowed from the two organisations for our earlier discussion.

The two sources of data on FDI provide two distinct sets of numbers. While the IMF provides data on FDI from the balance of payments statistics, UNCTAD provides data not only on FDI, but also on M&As by foreign companies, as well as their greenfield investments.[1]

This chapter will cover both the flows and stocks of FDI. While the former represents the investments that are made in a particular year, the latter allows us to assess the accumulation of FDI at the end of any year. Further, both inflows and outflows of FDI will be included in the discussion.

IMF Data on FDI and Related Forms of Investment

FDI statistics provided by the IMF follow the classifications given in BPM6. FDI is included as a component of the 'Financial

Account', the details of which are shown in Box 3.1. As can be seen, FDI belongs to a category of capital flows that includes portfolio and other investments, besides 'financial derivatives' and 'employee stock options' (ESO). Each of these categories of investments is used to settle external payments, as is the fourth component, namely 'reserve assets'.

Box 3.1: Financial Account of the Balance of Payments

- 3.1 Direct investment
  - 3.1.1 Equity and investment fund shares
    - 3.1.1.1 Equity other than reinvestment of earnings
    - 3.1.1.2 Reinvestment of earnings
  - 3.1.2 Debt instruments
- 3.2 Portfolio investment
  - 3.2.1 Equity and investment fund shares
  - 3.2.2 Debt securities
- 3.3 Financial derivatives (other than reserves) and employee stock options
- 3.4 Other investment
  - 3.4.1 Other equity
  - 3.4.2 Currency and deposits
  - 3.4.3 Loans
  - 3.4.4 Insurance, pension and standardised guarantee schemes
  - 3.4.5 Trade credit and advances
  - 3.4.6 Other accounts receivable/payable—other
  - 3.4.7 Special drawing rights
- 3.5 Reserve assets
  - 3.5.1 Monetary gold
  - 3.5.2 Special drawing rights
  - 3.5.3 Reserve position in the IMF
  - 3.5.4 Other reserve assets

Source: IMF (2009: Appendix 9).

We discussed earlier how direct investment and portfolio investment are both defined in BPM6. Here, we will briefly allude to the treatment of financial derivatives and ESOs and 'other investments'. BPM6 defines a financial derivative as a financial instrument, which is 'linked to another specific financial instrument or indicator or commodity and through which specific financial risks (such as interest rate risk, foreign exchange risk, equity and commodity price risks, credit risk, and so on) can be traded in their own right in financial markets' (IMF 2009: 93). ESOs are options to buy the shares of a company that are offered to employees of the company as remuneration or as an incentive package. ESOs can also be considered financial derivatives if the employees' stock options can be traded on financial markets without any restriction (ibid.: 96).

'Other investment', according to BPM6, is a residual category that includes investment flows not included in any of the other categories in the Financial Account, namely direct investment, portfolio investment, financial derivatives and ESOs, and reserve assets. It includes, 'other equity', which can 'include equity in quasi-corporations, such as branches, trusts, limited liability and other partnerships, unincorporated funds, and notional units for ownership of real estate and other natural resources' (ibid.: 85). These characterisations of the components of the Financial Account of the Balance of Payments indicate a close relationship between FDI, FPI and other investments (henceforth, 'FPI and others').

BPM6 defines 'reserve assets' as

> those external assets that are readily available to and controlled by monetary authorities for meeting balance of payments financing needs, for intervention in exchange markets to affect the currency exchange rate, and for other related purposes (such as maintaining confidence in the currency and the economy, and serving as a basis for foreign borrowing). (Ibid.: 111)

Estimates of Foreign Investment Flows

Our first objective is to provide estimates of the different forms of investment flows over the past four decades, which will also provide us a perspective of the relative importance of FDI in relation to the other forms of investment flows that the IMF includes in the Financial Account of the Balance of Payments.

Foreign investment inflows in overall terms increased from just over $22 billion in 1970 to over $4.6 trillion in 2016, while the corresponding figures for outflows were $26 billion and $5.6 trillion, respectively (Figure 3.1).

Figure 3.1 shows that the increases in foreign investment flows were not gradual; there were periods of rapid increase all through the period. After remaining well below the $100-billion mark, investment flows quickly crossed the $300-billion threshold in a significant upturn in the latter half of the 1970s, the increase being triggered by portfolio and other investment flows, which we can see in Table 3.1.

Figure 3.1: Foreign Investment Flows, 1970–2016

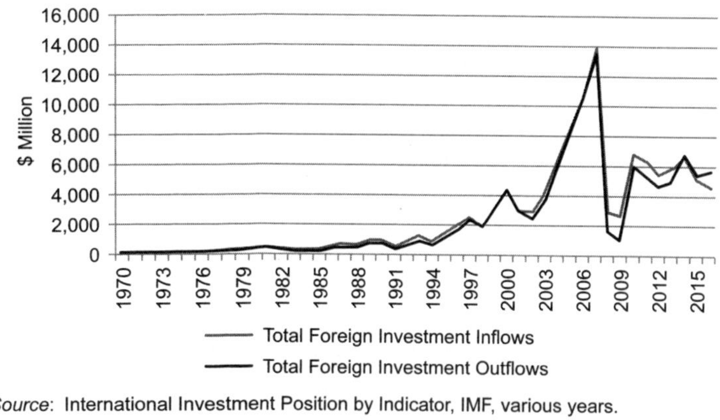

Source: International Investment Position by Indicator, IMF, various years.

After breaching the $400-billion level in the early 1980s, investment flows dipped as the global economy was subjected to the considerable stress caused by the first of the major financial crises in the post-Bretton Woods period, namely the developing-country debt crisis.

By the time the debt crisis went off the boil, global economic management was firmly in the control of the Bretton Woods twins,

Table 3.1: Inflows of Foreign Investment by Major Categories, 1970–2016 ($ Billion)

Categories	*Average for the Decades*				
	1970–79	*1980–89*	*1990–99*	*2000–09*	*2010–16*
Direct investment inflows	16.6	83.7	412.4	1,788.2	2,802.7
Portfolio investment inflows	19.8	120.8	645.0	2,605.7	2,182.2
Other investment inflows	88.0	283.9	505.9	1,517.3	866.4
Total investment inflows	124.4	488.4	1,563.3	5,911.2	5,851.3

Source: International Investment Position by Indicator, IMF, various years.

the IMF and World Bank, whose prescription for opening the capital account was accepted either *de jure* or *de facto* by almost all countries. No wonder, therefore, that investment flows surged in the early 1990s, and by 1994, they had reached close to the $1 trillion-mark.

Prior to the next big financial crisis that gripped East Asia in 1997, inflows peaked yet again, topping $2.5 trillion. A quick turnaround by the countries from the financial crisis helped check not only a global contagion, but also helped foreign investment flows scale the $4-trillion mark in the new millennium. A minor dip in flows coinciding with the uncertainties in Europe was followed by the strongest phase of expansion of foreign investment flows, resulting in inflows (as well as outflows) reaching astronomical levels. Between 2002 and 2007, both inward and outward investment flows increased by similar magnitudes: from about $3 trillion to nearly $14 trillion, a nearly five-fold increase within five years. Data for the decade of the 2010s shows that foreign investment flows have been struggling to reach the levels that they had in the previous decade.

Table 3.2 summarises the position of FDI *vis-à-vis* the other forms of investment flows during the period 1970–2016.

Table 3.2 shows the two features of the overall foreign investment flows. The first is the steep increase in foreign investment

Table 3.2: Outflows of Foreign Investment by Major Categories, 1970–2016 ($ Billion)

Categories	*Average for the Decades*				
	1970–79	*1980–89*	*1990–99*	*2000–09*	*2010–16*
Direct investment inflows	23.8	74.4	429.2	1,861.3	2,592.4
Portfolio investment inflows	10.6	62.1	498.7	1,860.3	1,645.4
Other investment inflows	74.0	227.1	388.1	1,396.9	1,191.9
Total investment inflows	108.4	363.6	1319.1	5,502.6	5,546.5

Source: International Investment Position by Indicator, IMF, various years.

flows, with a distinctly upward trend prominent since the 1980s. Until the 2000s, average investment flows, both inflows and outflows, increased nearly three-fold as compared to the immediately preceding decade. Thus, between the 1980s and the first decade of the new millennium, the average of the total inward investment flows had increased from less than $500 billion to nearly $6 trillion, or by a factor of 12. Outward investment flows increased somewhat higher, from nearly $360 billion to $5.5 trillion over the same period, or by a factor of 15. This phase of rapid increase was punctuated by the economic recession of 2008, following which there was a significant cooling of foreign investment flows.

A second aspect arises from putting the absolute numbers of foreign investment flows in perspective by comparing them with the global GDP. In the three decades since the 1980s, foreign investment inflows increased from a mere 3 per cent of global GDP to nearly 13 per cent (Table 3.3), while the corresponding numbers for outflows were less than 3 per cent and 12 per cent (Table 3.4). More significantly, when investment flows peaked in 2007, they were more than 24 per cent of the global GDP (Figure 3.2). These three insights inform us about the extent to which financialisation of the global economy has been taking place in recent decades.

Table 3.3: Foreign Investment Inflows and Global GDP, 1980s to 2010s

Decades	*Average for the Decades ($ Billion)*		*Foreign Investment Inflows as Share of GDP (%)*
	Global GDP	*Foreign Investment Inflows*	
1980s	14,172.5	488.4	3.4
1990s	28,326.7	1,563.3	5.5
2000s	46,453.1	5,911.2	12.7
2010s	70,235.1	5,851.3	8.3

Source: Foreign Direct Investment: Inward and Outward Flows and Stock, UNCTAD, various years; World Development Indicators, World Bank, various years.

Table 3.4: Foreign Investment Outflows and Global GDP, 1980s to 2010s

Decades	*Average for the Decades ($ Billion)*		*Foreign Investment Outflows as Share of GDP (%)*
	Global GDP	*Foreign Investment Outflows*	
1980s	14,172.5	363.6	2.6
1990s	28,326.7	1,319.1	4.7
2000s	46,453.1	5,502.6	11.8
2010s	70,235.1	5,546.5	7.9

Source: Foreign Direct Investment: Inward and Outward Flows and Stock, UNCTAD, various years; World Development Indicators, World Bank, various years.

Figure 3.2: Foreign Investment Inflows as a Share of GDP, 1970–2016 (%)

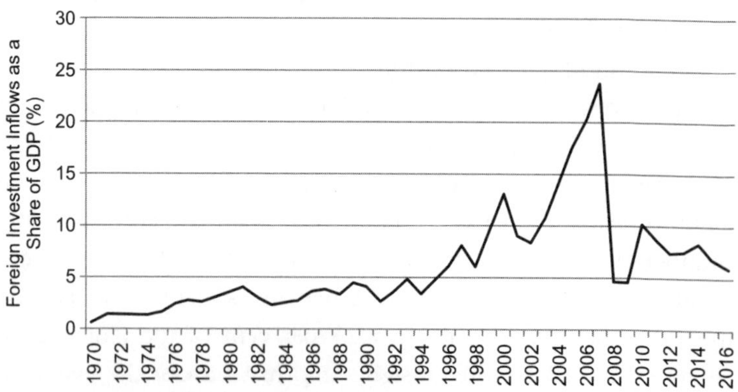

Source: Foreign Direct Investment: Inward and Outward Flows and Stock, UNCTAD, various years; World Development Indicators, World Bank, various years.

We shall now refer to Tables 3.1 and 3.2 to discuss the observed trends in the two larger forms of foreign investment flows, namely FDI and FPI, in recent years. Analytically, FDI is distinctly different from FPI, for the former, as we discussed earlier, is usually longer-term investment, while the latter is short-term, besides being the footloose and speculative form of investment. The behaviour of FDI and FPI over time necessitates, in our view, three sets of observations, which we shall briefly dwell on in the following paragraphs.

First, in most of the years referred to in Tables 3.1 and 3.2, FPI was the larger of the two forms of investments until the onset of the recession of 2008. Long-term investment, which complements the efforts of the recipient states to set up productive capacities, was really lagging FPI. In other words, the composition of foreign investments was driving a growing wedge between the financial and the real world. It was, therefore, hardly surprising that the financial system driven by booms and busts of FPI was able to expose the weak foundations of the real economy, resulting in recurring episodes of economic crises.[2]

Second, the data suggests that even within the overall domination by portfolio investment, there were signs of the growing importance of FDI. The rising trend was more pronounced in case of inflows, where the share of FDI increased from less than a sixth of the total inflows in the decade of the 1970s to a fourth in the 1990s and increased further to nearly half of the total flows in the 2010s. While in case of inflows, the share of FDI had maintained a continuous upward trend, reaching its highest share in the 2010s, the trend in the outflows saw an uneven pattern in the share of FDI, increasing to over 58 per cent in the previous decade, to settling at a level slightly below that of the share in inflows. This fact should be seen in light of an observation in Dunning and Dilyard (1999: 8) that 'some FDI is increasingly taking on the characteristics of FPI'.

It is interesting to note that the pattern displayed by FDI inflows in terms of its relative share corresponds with the changing narrative on the importance of FDI emphasised in the policy debates. It may be recalled, we had mentioned in Chapter 1, that from the 1960s, the US administration tried to curb FDI outflows from the country; this form of investment was somewhat more muted than the others. The inflows did not pick up significantly in the 1980s as major economies, including the US, were intervening in the first major financial crisis of the post-World War II era which took the form of the developing-country debt crisis. By the turn of the decade, the tide had turned decisively in favour of FDI for two reasons. First, foreign firms were encouraged to buy-out the debt of the developing countries through, what is better known as, debt-for-equity swaps. Second, with the advent of the Washington Consensus, liberalisation of FDI policies became one of the centrepieces of economic reforms that developing countries were advised to follow.[3]

Our third observation is related to an earlier point we made that FDI has a close relationship with FPI in that the sources of the two flows are related. Dunning and Dilyard (1999: 5–6) have argued that FDI and FPI have been closely linked from as early as the beginning of the nineteenth century and that there is 'growing interconnectedness between FDI and FPI'. This relationship between the two forms of capital has become significantly more complex since the end of the twentieth century.

If FDI and FPI are juxtaposed over the period for which we have the data, an interesting pattern emerges, which is captured in Figure 3.3. It lends itself to two observations. The first is that the cycles of FPI upswing are more pronounced than those of FDI. And the second is that the existence of an interesting relationship, especially between the cycles of FPI upswing and the global economic cycles, can be seen over the entire period.

Figure 3.3: Trends in FDI and FPI, and Other Investment Inflows, 1970–2016

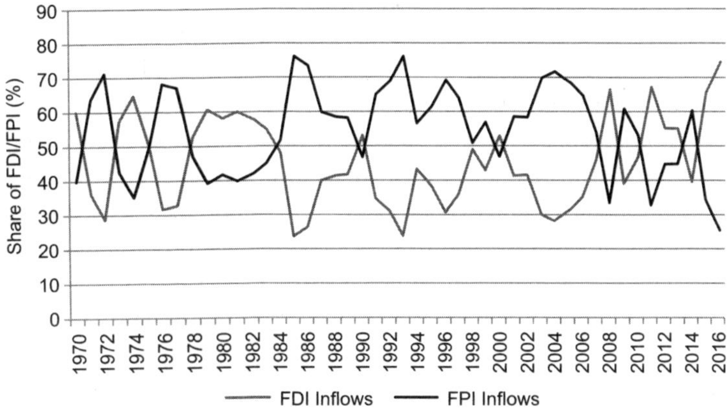

Source: International Investment Position by Indicator, IMF, various years.

The FPI upswings shown in Figure 3.3 are clearly followed by episodes of economic uncertainty. This lends weight to the argument that has been regularly made over the past decade that financialisation of the global economy has increased the downside. The data presented here shows that larger flows of FPI have had destabilising effects on the global economy. This is briefly enumerated here.

In the first half of the 1970s, FPI upswing came in the immediate aftermath of the breakdown of the Bretton Woods system, the post-World War II exchange rate management system that recognised the centrality of the US dollar.

The next episode of FPI upswing corresponded with the recycling of petrodollars. Following the oil price hike in 1973, the oil-rich countries registered huge current account surpluses, a large proportion of which was deposited in money-centre banks in the US. The banks, in turn, lent heavily to several developing countries, mostly in the Latin American region. By the early 1980s, the borrowers realised that they were unable to service the debt, and in 1984, sovereign debt default had almost become a reality. The US and the IMF brokered a series of rescheduling of debts, by creating what was euphemistically called 'new money'. This caused yet another upswing in the FPI during the mid- to late-1980s.

After a brief interlude, FPI went through a relatively long period of upswing, from 1992 to almost 1999, a period that saw two financial crises: the Mexican peso crisis in 1994 followed by the east Asian financial crisis in 1997. The latter was the first financial crisis that not only caused a global contagion, facilitated by a highly interconnected global economy, but also led to a significant cooling of the global economy.

Another short period of relative decline in the share of FPI *vis-à-vis* FDI that occurred during the economic uncertainties faced by both the US and Europe was followed by yet another prolonged spell of upswing of FPI during which the housing bubble in the US coupled with the subprime crisis sent the global economy spiralling into recession.

In the present decade, as the global economy has struggled to recover from the recession, the FDI–FPI patterns expectedly show no clear winners. These observations lend themselves to only one conclusion: excessive supplies of FPI result in serious uncertainties to the global economy. Therefore, regulation of this form of capital, identified aptly as 'unproductive capital', should be on top of the agenda of the global institutions.

Analysing the Components of FDI

We will now analyse the behaviour of the different components of FDI since 1970. Recall the definition of direct investment given by BPM6, according to which an FDI enterprise is one in which the foreign investor has 10 per cent or more of equity stake. The foreign investor is seen to have 'control' over the enterprise if its share in the equity stake is over 50 per cent, and when the equity stake is between 10 per cent and 50 per cent, the foreign investor has 'significant degree of influence'.

From the aforementioned definition, it is clear that equity-holding is a key component of FDI. There are two other components identified by BPM6, namely retained or reinvested earnings and debt instruments. Retained earnings of direct investment enterprises have become a prominent component of FDI. The undistributed part of net operating surplus, net property income and net current transfers is recorded as retained earnings or net saving of corporations. Retained earnings of direct investors are treated as if they were distributed to the owners, who then reinvest these earnings back into the enterprise. In terms of the settlement of this item on the account books, BPM6 clarifies that the 'imputation of income to the owners of investment funds and direct investors is shown in the primary income account as "reinvested earnings" and the corresponding flow is recorded in the financial account as "reinvestment of earnings"' (IMF 2009: 189). Reinvestment of earnings is an imputed financial transaction; it is not shown separately but is included implicitly in the total value of equity. From this it should be understood that reinvestment of earnings does not entail fresh infusion of capital from the foreign direct investors; these are their claims arising from profits of existing direct investment enterprises that they use to build their assets in their host countries. Thus, an increase in FDI on account of higher reinvestment of earnings does not arise from the inflows on the capital account; it results from the decisions by foreign investors in FDI enterprises not to repatriate their investment incomes.

Debt instrument transactions and positions are intercompany lending between enterprises that have 'direct investment' relationships. BPM6 clarifies that although debt and other similar 'claims that do not involve voting power are not relevant to defining a direct investment relationship, they are included in direct investment transactions and positions if a direct investment relationship exists between the parties' (ibid.: paragraph 6.27). Thus, all debt instruments, except for monetary gold, special drawing rights (SDRs), currency, interbank positions and pension and related entitlements can potentially be considered direct investment. However, transactions between affiliates in financial assets issued by unrelated third parties are not included as direct investment transactions. All debt positions between selected types of affiliated financial corporations that are not considered direct investment are included under portfolio or other investment.

From the data available for the reporting countries, FDI inflows increased from under $11 billion in 1970 to nearly $2.2 trillion in 2016. Figures 3.4 and 3.5 show the trends in the different categories of FDI inflows from 1970 to 2016.

Investments in the equity of enterprises have been the largest component of both FDI inflows and outflows since the 1980s, and were well above 50 per cent of the total flows during this period. In

Figure 3.4: Trends in FDI Inflows, 1970–2016

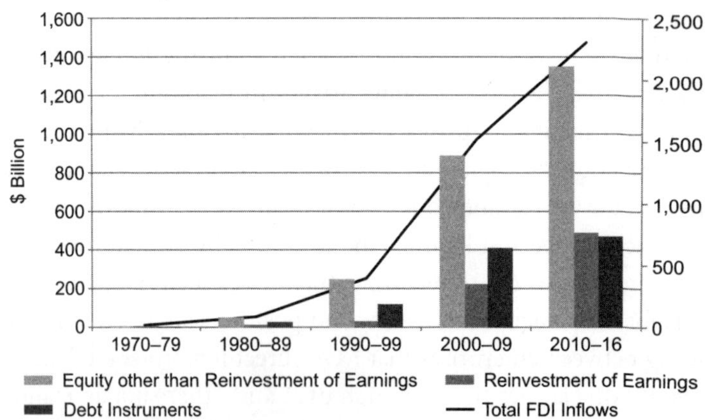

Source: International Investment Position by Indicator, IMF, various years.

Figure 3.5: Trends in FDI Outflows, 1970–2016

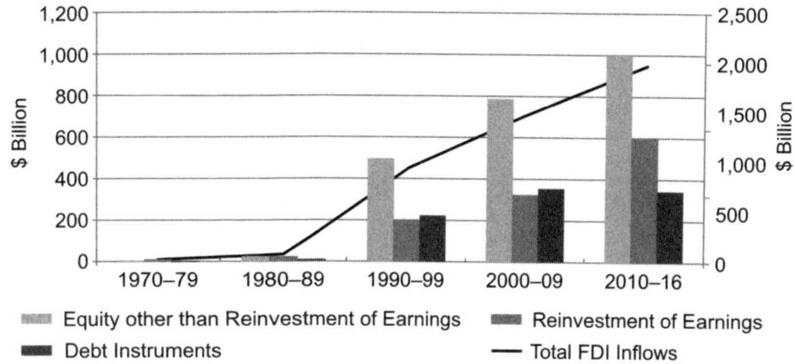

Source: International Investment Position by Indicator, IMF, various years.

the later decades, reinvestment of earnings was the less-preferred option exercised by direct investors to increase their presence in host economies. Taken without any additional qualification, this observation implies that the foreign investors have been infusing fresh capital in their host countries instead of expanding their presence by merely reinvesting their earnings. However, FDI data from IMF does not allow us to distinguish between investments in equity being made in a 'greenfield' or a 'brownfield' project. Therefore, the extent to which FDI has contributed to the fresh addition of productive capacities in the recipient economies cannot be readily assessed. (Tables 3.5 and 3.6).

Table 3.5: Components of Global FDI Inflows: Relative Shares, 1970–2016 (%)

Components	*Average for the Decades*				
	1970–79	*1980–89*	*1990–99*	*2000–09*	*2010–16*
Equity other than Reinvestment of Earnings	36.0	58.6	63.2	58.5	58.6
Reinvestment of Earnings	39.9	13.1	7.0	14.6	21.1
Debt Instruments	24.1	28.3	29.8	26.9	20.3
Total	100.0	100.0	100.0	100.0	100.0

Source: International Investment Position by Indicator, IMF, various years.

Table 3.6: Components of Global FDI Outflows: Relative Shares, 1970–2016 (%)

Components	*Average for the Decades*				
	1970–79	*1980–89*	*1990–99*	*2000–09*	*2010–16*
Equity other than Reinvestment of Earnings	21.8	45.4	53.8	53.6	51.5
Reinvestment of Earnings	49.8	36.9	21.9	22.2	30.8
Debt Instruments	28.4	17.7	24.3	24.2	17.7
Total	100.0	100.0	100.0	100.0	100.0

Source: International Investment Position by Indicator, IMF, various years.

Disaggregating FDI Flows

The most extensively used source for disaggregated data is the UNCTAD database, which provides data on FDI flows since 1970. This database includes data for associates and subsidiaries of foreign firms, including 'net sales of shares and loans (including non-cash acquisitions made against equipment, manufacturing rights, etc.) to the parent company plus the parent firm's share of the affiliate's reinvested earnings plus total net intra-company loans (short- and long-term) provided by the parent company'. For branches of foreign companies, data on FDI flows captures the 'increase in reinvested earnings plus the net increase in funds received from the foreign direct investor' (UNCTAD, n.d.).

In addition, UNCTAD provides data on two analytically important components of FDI, namely M&A and 'greenfield' investments. However, the data on these categories is available for fewer years as compared to the overall figures on FDI.

UNCTAD informs us that the inflows of FDI increased from $13 billion in 1970 to $1.7 trillion in 2016. Inflows had increased to over $1.9 trillion in 2015, the highest ever, but declined in the two subsequent years.

According to the UNCTAD, FDI inflows increased continuously until the year 2000, buoyed by steep rise in inflows to the developed countries in the closing years of the 1990s. After the global economy overcame the uncertainties in the early 2000s, FDI inflows found the highest level for that period as the 2008 recession was setting in (Figure 3.6). The revival of inflows following the recession took place as developing countries emerged as the more preferred destinations for direct investors (Figure 3.7). Between 2009 and 2014, the share of developing countries in the total inflows increased from 40 to 53 per cent; but there was some shift in the pattern thereafter. In this context, it should also be pointed out that China has been a key factor influencing the rise in the developing-country share. In recent years, China's contribution has usually been close to a fifth of the FDI inflows to the developing countries.

Figure 3.6: Inflows of FDI, 1970–2017 ($ Billion)

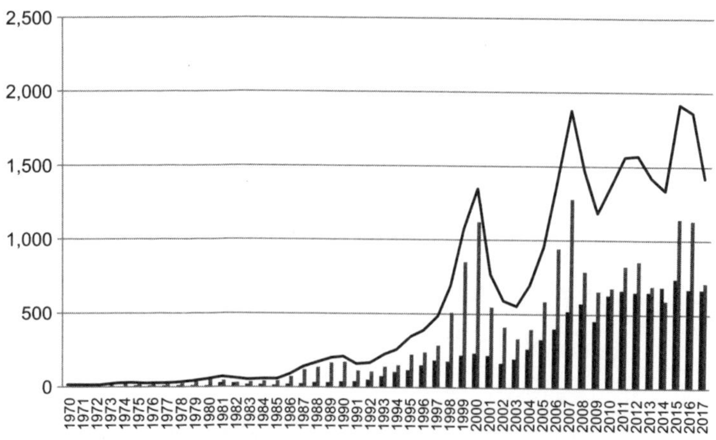

Source: Foreign Direct Investment: Inward and Outward Flows and Stock, UNCTAD, various years.

Figure 3.7 also shows the cyclical nature of FDI inflows: strong surge towards one group of countries was followed by a reversal of almost equal magnitude. There are two prominent cycles of FDI surge towards developing countries: the first in the early 1980s, just prior to debt crisis, and again in the 1990s, preceding the east Asian financial crisis. However, the sharp reversals faced by the developing countries after these surges and the adverse impact on their growth momentum raise serious questions whether FDI inflows have positively impacted their economies. Some more evidence in support of this proposition is presented in a subsequent discussion.

Despite the emergence of developing countries like China and India as major recipients of FDI, developed countries have remained the preferred destinations of direct investors by a small margin in recent years, as Figure 3.7 shows.

Figure 3.7: FDI Inflows to the Developed and Developing Countries, 1970–2017 ($ Billion)

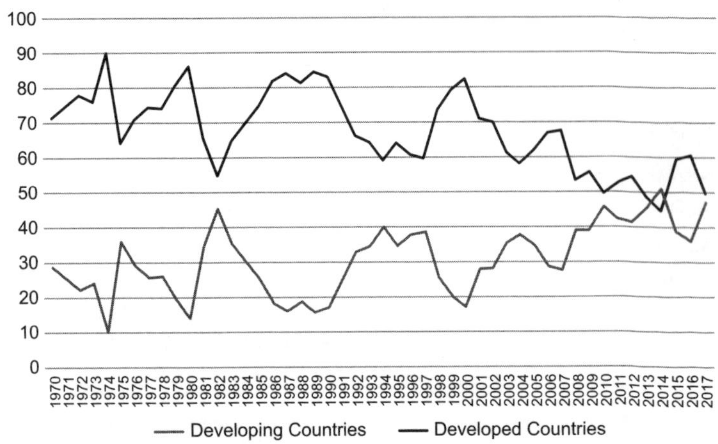

Source: Foreign Direct Investment: Inward and Outward Flows and Stock, UNCTAD, various years.

FDI inflows have remained concentrated in a few economies (Table 3.7). The top-10 recipients have accounted for more than half of the average inflows during the 2010s. Over the decades, the composition of the major destinations has changed quite drastically, several developing countries, including China, Brazil and India, having emerged among the top destinations.

The increasing share of developing countries raises an interesting question regarding the distribution of the gains from FDI inflows. We have already pointed to the disproportionately large share of China in the inflows to developing countries, but when the inflows to the poorer countries are observed, the reality of FDI inflows becomes quite evident. There is still no evidence that FDI has been able to pull these countries by their bootstraps.

Table 3.7: Top Recipients of FDI, 1970–2017 ($ Billion)

Host Countries	*Average for the Decades*				
	1970–79	*1980–89*	*1990–99*	*2000–09*	*2010–17*
United States	3.2	33.7	89.1	174.5	278.5
China	—	1.6	29.0	68.6	127.2
Hong Kong SAR	0.3	2.1	9.0	38.2	102.6
Brazil	1.3	1.7	9.9	24.0	71.0
Singapore	0.3	1.9	9.0	20.4	61.3
Netherlands	1.0	2.7	15.4	38.5	43.9
France	1.4	4.1	23.0	26.1	28.6
Australia	1.0	3.9	5.9	20.1	46.0
Switzerland, Liechtenstein	—	1.2	4.4	17.9	33.4
India	0.0	0.1	1.5	16.1	34.9
Total	8.5	53.1	196.3	444.4	827.4

Source: Foreign Direct Investment: Inward and Outward Flows and Stock, UNCTAD, various years.

Table 3.8 provides the inflow data of developing countries classified by their levels of incomes. The lower-middle income countries are not included separately in the table as several countries in this grouping were low-income countries not even a decade previously.

Table 3.8: Share of Developing Country Groups in Global FDI Inflows, 1970–2016

Country Categories	*Average for the Decades*				
	1970–79	*1980–89*	*1990–99*	*2000–09*	*2010–16*
Upper-middle income developing economies	16.2	21.1	26.2	27.1	36.2
Middle-income developing economies	7.5	3.8	4.2	4.5	6.9
Low-income developing economies	1.1	0.3	0.3	0.5	1.3
All developing countries	24.5	25.2	30.6	32.1	44.4

Note: The categories are according to the World Bank classification.

Source: Foreign Direct Investment: Inward and Outward Flows and Stock, UNCTAD, various years.

Upper-middle income developing countries absorbed more than 80 per cent of the total FDI inflows to the developing world, a share that has remained so from the 1980s. In contrast, the middle- and low-income developing countries lost their shares during most decades since the 1970s. From these figures, an important observation can be made regarding the significance of the open-door policies followed by all countries to attract FDI. If the policy framework is the single most important determinant of FDI inflows, as it is made out to be, every country-grouping should have seen FDI inflows increase by similar magnitudes. That there are major variations suggests that there are some other factors making one group of countries more attractive than the others.

These observations are further reinforced by the regional distribution of FDI inflows captured in Table 3.9.

Table 3.9: Regional Distribution of FDI Inflows, 1970–2016 (% Share of Total Inflows)

Country Categories	*Average for the Decades*				
	1970–79	*1980–89*	*1990–99*	*2000–09*	*2010–16*
Africa	5.3	2.6	1.9	3.5	4.4
Developing Americas	11.1	8.2	9.1	7.8	11.2
Developing Asia	7.8	14.3	19.6	20.7	28.6
North America*	25.7	39.5	23.0	18.9	18.7
Europe	43.2	30.4	41.7	42.1	28.7

Note: * US and Canada.

Source: Foreign Direct Investment: Inward and Outward Flows and Stock, UNCTAD, various years.

FDI inflows have been considerably skewed across regions. Until the previous decade, nearly two-thirds of the inflows were concentrated in Europe and North America, and when Asia was added, the share went up to nearly four-fifths. Even within Asia, the same spectre of concentration can be seen, with the two relatively developed regions, namely East and Southeast Asia, attracting more than 80 per cent of the inflows. The contrast is provided by Africa: the region was attracting more direct investment in the 1970s than it had been able to after the region embraced open-door policies to FDI in keeping with the prescription of the Washington Consensus. The message conveyed by these numbers spread over four decades is quite unambiguous: relatively advanced regions would attract more FDI, notwithstanding the attractiveness of the FDI policies adopted by the governments.

This conclusion is supported by yet another indicator that the UNCTAD database provides, the share of FDI in the gross capital formation of the recipient countries.

The figures in Table 3.10 provide a complete picture of the importance of FDI in the capital formation of the country-groupings. For most groups, FDI inflows were well below 10 per cent of their

Table 3.10: Share of FDI Inflows in Gross Capital Formation, 1970–2016

Country Categories	*Average for the Decades*				
	1970–79	*1980–89*	*1990–99*	*2000–09*	*2010–16*
High-income developing economies*	2.4	3.3	8.2	11.9	8.4
Middle-income developing economies*	2.7	1.9	5.4	8.0	7.4
Low-income developing economies*	3.1	1.6	4.8	10.8	15.8
All developing economies	2.5	2.9	7.7	11.2	7.1
Developed economies**	1.6	2.5	5.1	9.4	7.3
World	0.0	2.6	5.7	10.0	7.3

Note: * World Bank definition; ** UN definition.

Source: Foreign Direct Investment: Inward and Outward Flows and Stock, UNCTAD, various years.

gross capital formation. This implies that although FDI inflows have risen considerably since the 2000s, there is no visible impact of these inflows on the capital formation of most country-groupings. In case of the sole exception, the low-income countries, the shares are much larger, since the somewhat large inflows they received, especially since 2010, were accompanied by significantly lower rates of capital formation as compared to most other groups.

This raises questions about the quality of FDI inflows: in Chapter 5, we shall provide evidence of this using Indian data.

Outflows of FDI

Outflows of FDI have been wholly dependent on developed countries, barring in the 2010s, when emerging economies began making their contributions, thus closing the gap (Figure 3.8). Developing countries became a consistent source of this form of capital during this decade. Their share reached a high of nearly 38 per cent in 2014 due to a sudden surge from the Hong Kong Special Administrative Region (SAR), but was soon reversed.

Figure 3.8: Outflows of FDI, 1970–2017

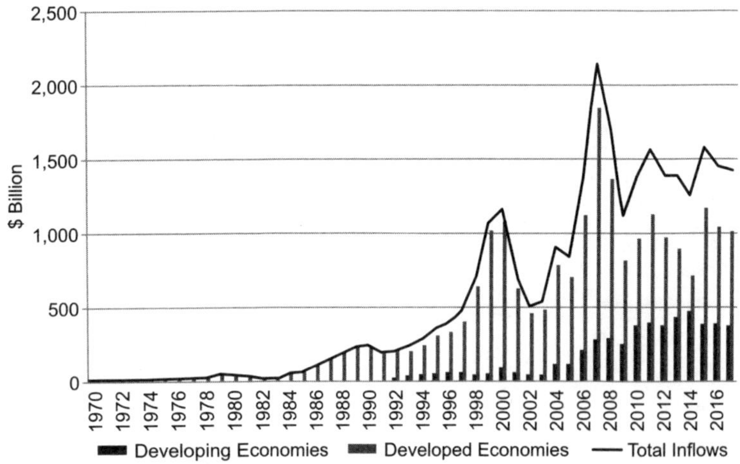

Source: Foreign Direct Investment: Inward and Outward Flows and Stock, UNCTAD, various years.

China's emergence as a provider of direct investment has been the most notable development since the later years of the 2000s. From a share of less than 2 per cent in 2005, China's share in the global FDI outflows increased to nearly 13 per cent by 2016, which was nearly 50 per cent of the outflows from the developing world.

China's emergence as a top investor country is the most remarkable piece of evidence in Table 3.11. Outward FDI from China had reached over $4 billion in the early years of the 1990s, but after the east Asian financial crisis in 1997, its outflows shrank to below $1 billion. However, from 2005, outward FDI consistently increased, reaching almost $200 billion in 2016.

Another interesting trend is the emergence of Hong Kong SAR, in the list of the top-10 providers of FDI. It may be pointed out that Hong Kong has had a close relationship with the mainland, especially after the British withdrawal from its former colony in 1997 and Beijing's recognition of it as an SAR. Thus, the two regions of China have emerged as the largest providers of FDI after the US (Table 3.11).

Table 3.11: Top Sources of FDI, 1970–2016

Investor Countries	*Average for the Decades*				
	1970–79	*1980–89*	*1990–99*	*2000–09*	*2010–16*
United States	12.4	17.5	86.9	205.6	309.5
Japan	1.6	14.4	25.1	53.4	124.1
China	n/a	0.5	2.3	18.8	116.1
United Kingdom	4.6	16.6	57.4	124.4	5.9
Hong Kong SAR	n/a	1.2	16.7	38.4	85.7
Germany	n/a	n/a	43.1	64.2	81.2
Canada	1.4	4.4	12.9	43.1	59.8
British Virgin Islands	n/a	1.7	2.9	28.8	69.9
France	1.1	6.4	39.9	73.9	47.5
Luxembourg	n/a	n/a	n/a	15.9	36.7

Source: Foreign Direct Investment: Inward and Outward Flows and Stock, UNCTAD, various years.

Main Observations

We pointed out in an earlier discussion that the importance of FDI grew after developing countries began adopting the policies of economic liberalisation from the 1980s. The openness of these economies began to get reflected in their increasing shares; in the 2010s, foreign direct investors showed no clear preferences between developed and developing countries. Emerging economies like China, Brazil and India tipped the scales in favour of the developing countries.

Developed countries remained the predominant providers of FDI, although in the decade of the 2010s, China has emerged as a major source.

Notes

1. Inter-governmental agencies normally provide data from official sources. One of the rare exceptions is UNCTAD's reporting of M&As and greenfield investments, for which the agency relies on non-official sources.

2. Patnaik (2016) calls this 'illusionism of finance', a situation in which 'all that matters is the soundness of the financial calculation, not the state of the real economy or the possible future travails of the real economy'.

3. Williamson (2004: 8) put this in a rather straightforward manner: 'Barriers impeding the entry of foreign [direct investment] should be abolished.'

References

Dunning, John and John Dilyard. 1999. 'Towards a General Paradigm of Foreign Direct and Foreign Portfolio Investment'. *Transnational Corporations* 8 (1), April: 1–52.

IMF. 2009. 'Balance of Payments and International Investment Position Manual', sixth edition. Washington, D. C.

_____. (various years). International Investment Position by Indicator: Liabilities, Direct Investment. Available at http://data.imf.org/regular.aspx?key=62805745 (accessed 15 July 2019).

Patnaik, Prabhat. 2016. 'The Illusionism of Finance'. Available at http://www.networkideas.org/wp-content/uploads/2016/10/Illusionism_Finance.pdf (accessed 10 June 2018).

UNCTAD (n.d.). 'Sources and Definitions'. Available at http://unctad.org/en/Pages/DIAE/FDI%20Statistics/Sources-and-Definitions.aspx (accessed 15 June 2018).

_____. (various years). 'Foreign Direct Investment: Inward and Outward Flows and Stock, Annual'. *UNCTADStat*. Available at https://unctadstat.unctad.org/wds/TableViewer/tableView.aspx?ReportId=96740 (accessed 15 June 2018).

Williamson, John. 2004. 'The Washington Consensus as Policy Prescription for Development'. Lecture in the series 'Practitioners of Development', delivered at the World Bank, 13 January. Available at https://piie.com/publications/papers/williamson0204.pdf (accessed 20 June 2018).

World Bank (various years). 'World Development Indicators'. Available at https://databank.worldbank.org/reports.aspx?source=world-development-indicators (accessed 20 July 2018).

four

India's Policies towards FDI

India's foreign investment policies have evolved from restricting participation of foreign companies in the early post-Independence days to the adoption of open-door policies over the past few decades. Such has been the extent of liberalisation that Government of India has claimed that 'India is now the world's most open economy for foreign investment' (Government of India 2018a).[1] Foreign investment policies were liberalised from the mid-1980s, even before the adoption of economic reforms in 1991.

This chapter will discuss the evolution of India's FDI policies over the past seven decades in two broad sections, the first dealing with the pre-reforms phase and the second, the decades since 1991.

FDI Policies in the Pre-1991 Decades

It has often been argued that the Indian government went from a phase of hostility towards foreign investment in the early post-Independence decades, which changed since the 1980s (Martinussen 1988). However, we shall argue that this characterisation of India's foreign investment policies was not entirely substantiated by the policy pronouncements that were made in this phase.

The first substantive policy pronouncement in which the government dwelled on the role of foreign capital in the economy was the Industrial Policy Statement (IPS), presented in April 1948. IPS argued that foreign capital was valuable in bringing resources for development and that it also provided technology and knowledge for rapid industrialisation of India. However, the IPS of 1948 did not provide clear assurances or guarantees to foreign capital operating in India, for it said that the 'conditions under which they may participate should be carefully regulated in national interest'. It was further stated that foreign capital would be regulated under a new legislation that would provide for 'scrutiny and approval by the Central Government of every individual case of participation of foreign capital and management in industry'.

It seems that the government did a quick rethink of its stance towards foreign capital, and this was reflected in Prime Minister Jawaharlal Nehru's statement to Parliament on foreign investment in 1949.[2] While the IPS had stated that 'as a rule major interest in ownership and effective control should always be in Indian hands', the prime minister opined that there can be no hard and fast rule in this matter. His statement clarified that the '... Government would not object to foreign capital having control of a concern for a limited period ...'. There was a similar turnaround on the question of control in Indian hands. The prime minister remarked that the government would not object to the employment of non-Indians in posts requiring technical skills and experience when Indians of requisite qualifications were not available, as long as the foreign enterprises attached vital importance to the training and employment of Indians for such positions in the quickest manner. He further explained that India, with a low level of domestic savings rate, needed foreign capital to undertake larger investments for rapid industrialisation. The statement that foreign private capital was also important because 'in many cases scientific, technical and industrial knowledge and capital equipment can best be secured along with foreign capital' was surprisingly similar to the thinking of the governments in the post-reforms phase. The prime minister also assured foreign capital that the government:

1. did not intend to place any restriction or impose conditions which were not applicable to similar Indian enterprises;
2. would also frame their policy to enable further foreign capital to be invested in India on terms and conditions that were mutually advantageous;
3. did not foresee any difficulty in remittance of profits;
4. had no intention of placing any restriction on withdrawal of foreign capital investments; and
5. would pay compensation on a fair and equitable basis in case of compulsory acquisition of any foreign concern.

In other words, he assured that foreign investments would be protected in India and that they could freely repatriate their profits and divest from India. Such assurances have formed the core of the investment promotion and protection treaties that the government has signed since the 1990s (Dhar, Joseph and James 2012).

Government's policies on the role and responsibilities of foreign capital during the 1950s and early 1960s were summed up in its press note of May 1961:

> Basically, the policy regarding foreign investments would be to attract private foreign capital in those fields, in which the country needs to develop in pursuance of the Plan targets. While Government have been encouraging the investment of private foreign capital in the country, it is to be recognized that this has necessarily to be on a selective basis.
>
> If any project is approved for development in the private sector and, if imported plant and machinery are required, foreign capital investment would ordinarily be welcome as a form of financing the project. While Indian majority holding would be generally welcome, the ratio of foreign capital in joint venture enterprises,

> the extent of foreign shareholding that is to be permitted in any case etc., have necessarily to be judged on merits. This judgment is made after evaluating the technical skills offered and after weighing the requirements of foreign exchange for the purchase of equipment from abroad and the desire of Indian collaborators to play an effective part in the company's management. (Kust 1964: 142)

Thus, the government invited foreign capital to participate in India, but its participation was to be dictated by the country's development priorities.

The foreign exchange crisis of the mid-1960s brought renewed thinking in the government on the role of foreign capital. The Mudaliar Committee on Foreign Collaboration (Government of India 1967), in its report in 1967, made several major recommendations, which included:

1. positive approach to the import of know-how, particularly of process know-how, or product design;
2. favourable attitude towards joint ventures involving foreign equity participation in industries, as they are beneficial as far as the government's policy allowing foreign capital participation and substantial import of capital goods are concerned; and
3. liberal approach towards foreign collaborations in substantially export-oriented industries.

Accepting the Mudaliar Committee's recommendations and for minimising the procedural delays in dealing with applications relating to foreign investment and collaboration, the government established the Foreign Investment Board[3] in 1968. In January 1969, the government issued three illustrative lists of industries where, in keeping with the foreign investment policy, (a) financial collaboration was permitted, (b) only technical collaboration was permitted and (c) no collaboration was considered necessary. This step helped in lending considerable transparency to the policy framework.

The next big move of the government was to introduce FERA in 1973. FERA required companies with foreign shareholding to reduce the share of the foreign investors to 40 per cent in an enterprise for it to be treated at par with an Indian company. There were some exceptions to this general rule: for companies using high technologies and/or exporting 40 per cent of their own production, foreign investors' shareholding could be as high as 74 per cent (Dhar 1988: 26). This implied that after the dilution of foreign equity, a company even with (substantial) foreign ownership could expand its operations like any other Indian company.

There is a view that FERA regulations were against the interests of foreign investors, since their shareholding in the companies they had invested in had to be reduced to a less-than majority level and that 'FERA' companies were subjected to strict controls (Joshi and Little 1996: 195). But, was FERA really an instrument of controlling operations of foreign companies in India? In the following discussion, we will provide evidence to show that FERA did not dilute the effective control of the foreign investors in the companies they had invested in. Moreover, it needs to be understood that FERA was, in effect, a regulation for limiting foreign exchange outflows from the country, and not one for regulating foreign investment in the country.[4]

The first point that needs to be understood is that India's foreign investment policies assumed a fair degree of transparency after the enactment of FERA. This was because it was FERA that made a clear distinction between an 'Indian' and a 'foreign' company by laying down the 40 per cent threshold in foreign shareholding for distinguishing the two, which had not existed earlier. Thus, companies with 40 per cent foreign shareholdings were treated as Indian companies and could expand their operations in India, while foreign shareholders continued to 'control' the enterprise as before. In the Chapter 2, we discussed that the global benchmark for identifying a foreign-controlled company was already veering towards the 10 per cent foreign shareholding when FERA was enacted.

Another interesting evidence is that at least a decade before the enactment of FERA, a guidebook of the US Department of Commerce for American investors informed prospective investors that 'some foreign firms consider corporate control as an essential condition for their entry into the Indian market' and 'in such cases they frequently take 40 per cent of shares' in the joint venture (US Department of Commerce 1963: 12). This implies that the foreign companies were willing to operate with less risk capital at stake in a joint venture, since they could exercise effective control over such an enterprise with less-than majority in equity capital.

The enactment of FERA did not result in the reduction of the dollar value of foreign investment in India; foreign investors were merely required to reduce their relative shares in their invested enterprises. This intention of the government was stated in a 1972 policy that introduced the so-called 'dilution formula' (Ganesan 1982: 5–7). The policy of inducting domestic equity in foreign-majority companies was strengthened in 1972. Till then, the extent of dilution by foreign-majority companies was done by examining each case individually, and to overcome the long delays caused by this procedure, it was decided to introduce the 'dilution formula'. According to this formula, whenever a foreign-majority company undertook an expansion programme, it was required to issue a certain share of fresh equity to Indians. A company having 75 per cent or more of foreign equity was required to issue 40 per cent of the additional equity to Indians. Companies having foreign equity between 60 and 75 per cent were required to issue a third of their new equity to Indians, and all the other foreign-majority companies were required to issue a fourth of their issue to Indians. FERA was an extension of the 'dilution policy'. Companies having more than 40 per cent foreign shareholding diluted their shares to comply with FERA and, in a large number of cases, several wholly owned subsidiaries and branches of foreign companies expanded their equity capital after keeping them unchanged for a long time (ibid.). Thus, these companies expanded their operations, raising them significantly above their pre-FERA levels (Chaudhuri 1979).

The 1980s saw the stage being set for sweeping liberalisation of foreign investment policies. The IPS of 1980 allowed 100 per cent export-oriented units, and these units were freed from the requirements of FERA.[5] Export-oriented units were established for encouraging foreign investment; these units were not subjected to import controls.

Foreign investment was allowed in some of the sunrise sectors. The communications industry, earlier reserved for the public sector, was opened for foreign investors, who could own up to 49 per cent of the total equity in an enterprise. The electronics industry was also opened, and the reason given by the government for free technology imports was that the Indian industry had to be competitive internationally. Import duties on components were reduced to help the Indian industry develop its competitive edge (BM 1984).

Thus, in the initial decades after the attainment of political independence, the government viewed foreign investment as a provider not only of the much-needed capital to a capital-short country, but also as a provider of critical inputs like technology and managerial skills. Within the broad sweep of policies that the government adopted, some policies like FERA did appear to be overly regulating foreign investors, but as pointed to earlier, this regulation eventually provided clarity to the foreign investors to expand their operations in the country.

Thus, in the 1980s, foreign investment policies were adopted to explicitly support the expansion of India's manufacturing base in several key sectors, notably automobiles, telecommunications and computer hardware. This set the tone for an open-door policy towards foreign investment, which came in the early 1990s as a part of the overall policy package that introduced economic liberalisation.

Foreign Investment Policies: Post-1991

A radical shift in India's foreign investment policy was seen immediately after the pro-reforms government of P. V. Narasimha Rao took office. The broad thrust of India's policy towards foreign investment was underlined by the then finance minister, Manmohan Singh, in his first budget speech:

> After four decades of planning for industrialisation, we have now reached a stage of development where we should welcome, rather than fear, foreign investment ... Direct foreign investment would provide access to capital, technology and markets. It would expose our industrial sector to competition from abroad in a phased manner. Cost, efficiency, and quality would begin to receive the attention they deserve. (Government of India 1991a: paragraph 12)

Singh also spelt out the pathway towards opening the door to foreign investors:

> First, direct foreign investment in specified high priority industries, with a raised limit for foreign equity at 51 per cent, would be given prompt approval, if equity inflows are sufficient to finance the import of capital goods at the stage of investment and if dividends are balanced by export earnings over a period of time. Second, foreign equity up to 51 per cent would be allowed for trading companies primarily engaged in export activities. Third, a

> special board would be constituted to negotiate with several large international firms and to approve direct foreign investment in selected areas; this would be a special regime to attract substantial investment that would provide access to high technology and to world markets. (Ibid.)

This statement introduced an important concept in India's policymaking framework, namely the concept of direct foreign investment or FDI.[6] Hitherto, the policies made a reference to the more general concept of 'foreign investment', but the new regime made a more pointed reference to FDI with clear emphasis on obtaining 'high technology' and access to world markets.

Government of India's changed policies towards foreign investment were reflected in the Statement of Industrial Policy 1991:

> Foreign investment would bring attendant advantages of technology transfer, marketing expertise, introduction of modern managerial techniques and new possibilities for promotion of exports. This is particularly necessary in the changing global scenario of industrial and economic cooperation marked by mobility of capital. The government will therefore welcome foreign investment which is in the interest of the country's industrial development. (Government of India 1991b: paragraph 24)

However, one of the important elements of the previous policy regime, namely 'dividend balancing' by foreign companies, remained: '... the payment of dividends would be monitored through the Reserve Bank of India so as to ensure that outflows on account of dividend payments are balanced by export earnings over a period of time' [ibid.: paragraph b(ii)]. In his budget speech in 1992–93, Singh had made it amply clear that the stance of the government towards foreign investment had decisively changed:

> Concern is sometimes expressed that the policy of welcoming foreign investment will hurt Indian industry and may jeopardise our sovereignty. These fears are misplaced. We must not remain

> permanent captives of a fear of the East India Company, as if nothing has changed in the past 300 years! India as a nation is capable of dealing with foreign investors on its own terms. Indian industry has also come of age and is now ready to enter a phase where it can both compete with foreign investment and cooperate with it. This is the trend all over the world and we cannot afford to be left out ... [W]e have enough policy instruments at our disposal to ensure that enterprises with foreign equity function in accordance with our national priorities. (Government of India 1992a: paragraph 22)

As a first step, it was proposed to raise the limit for foreign equity in specified high-priority industries to 51 per cent and to give 'prompt approval' to such investment proposals in 35 sectors (Government of India 1991b: Annexure III). This was the beginning of the eventual lifting of government scrutiny of foreign investment proposals.

Alongside, the government used the Statement of Industrial Policy to announce that it could establish a 'Special Empowered Board constituted to negotiate with a number of large international firms and approve direct foreign investment in select areas'. The Foreign Investment Promotion Board (FIPB) was established subsequently 'to attract substantial investment that would provide access to high technology and world markets'. The government also announced that 'investment programmes of such firms would be considered in totality, free from pre-determined parameters or procedures' (ibid.: 10). Yet another measure adopted by the government to dilute regulatory controls came in the form of withdrawal of the 'dividend balancing' requirements 'in all foreign investment approvals except for industries in the consumer goods sector' (Government of India 1992b).

In a further relaxation of FDI policies, foreign investors were invited in the power sector and hydrocarbon sectors, where, in the government's view, 'capacities are inadequate and needs for investments are large'. Proposals were invited for foreign investment, 'in production, refining and marketing of oil and gas, with a view to maximising the growth potential of this crucial area' (Government of India 1993). In 1997, automatic approval was granted to foreign investment proposals in 111 sectors 'involving foreign equity capital of upto 51% in the Indian Company' (Government of India 1996). This was the first major expansion of the list of sectors that were put on the automatic approval route.

In the year 2000, all sectors, except for a negative list, were placed under the automatic approval route for foreign investment. In the earlier regime, the dividend-balancing requirement was also completely removed (Government of India 2000a). But what was more important was that caps on equity holding by foreign investors were gradually raised in several sectors/activities. The key sectors which were opened for FDI were insurance and defence (see Box 4.1 for the government's justification for FDI in defence). In both these sectors, FDI was allowed, subject to a cap of 26 per cent (Government of India 2000b, 2001, 2002). In other sectors that were already open for foreign investment, the caps were increased. For instance, the cap for telecom services was increased from 49 to 74 per cent (Press Note No. 5 of 2005) by the United Progressive Alliance (UPA) government that followed. FDI was allowed up to 51 per cent in single-brand retail (Government of India 2006a).

Box 4.1: Discussion Paper of the DIPP FDI in the Defence Sector: Some Observations

- The indigenous R&D has not kept pace with the requirements and manufacture through transfer of technology (ToT) to Public Sector Units (PSUs)/Ordnance Factories (OFs) has proved to be ineffective and slow. ToT was often not complete, as the suppliers were more keen to push their own products, rather than indigenising the production in India.
- Since it may take some time for domestic companies to acquire a technical edge in the defence industry which is highly capital and technology intensive, it is necessary to access the technology through FDI.

(Contd)

Box 4.1 (Contd)

- The general perception is that the present minority FDI cap of 26% discourages original equipment manufacturers (OEMs) from bringing in proprietary technology, as OEMs are reluctant to license their proprietary technology.
- A higher FDI limit would ... provide a significant incentive for transfer of know-how/technology to the country, leading to higher levels of technological expertise.
- Increase of cap from 26% to 49% will not give any additional say to the foreign investor in the affairs of the company as per the provisions of the Company Law.
- By merely increasing the limit from 26% to 49% we may be accused by posterity of doing too little and too late. Therefore, in case we really want to have the state of the art technology, we have to permit anything above 50% if not 100%. It may be, therefore, desirable to allow either 100% or 74% as in the case of telecom sector.
- FDI provides the necessary supplemental funds and higher levels of foreign investment would reduce the corresponding fund requirements of the Indian partners.
- Defence manufacture is much more dispersed among larger number of countries today than in the past. Also, the ownership structure of many of the important defence production companies is in a state of continuous flux. Therefore, there is no risk of exclusive dependence on a particular country for investment and technology.
- Further, any such threat can be addressed with Government having a right to expropriate a manufacturing facility if the situation warrants.
- A large share of Indian foreign exchange goes towards defence purchases. Allowing more FDI in defence would result in significant savings in foreign exchange, as more foreign companies will establish defence industries in India.
- Liberalisation of the FDI regime would strengthen India's export potential by way of exports of defence products to other countries.
- Production of military equipment within the country will provide impetus to the manufacturing sector through large scale ancillarisation as in the case of major industrialised nations like USA, France and Germany.
- A large number of manufacturers of defence and dual-use products are finding it difficult to manage their production in western countries due to increasing costs of labour and other inputs. This is the right time for India to project itself as a new hub for manufacturing.
- A number of global defence majors are waiting to set up an alternative/additional manufacturing base in India. It is, therefore, not at all necessary for us to underwrite production. The FDI policy will not interfere with the prerogative of the Armed Forces to choose an equipment of their choice.
- There need not be any commitment on procurement and foreign investors will have to participate in the RFP (Requests for Proposals for sourcing of defence equipment) to technically qualify and also compete in the financial bid.
- For future RFP's by MoD, a condition may be imposed that the successful bidder would have to set up the system integration facility in India with a certain minimum percentage of value addition in India. The successful bidder should be allowed to bring equity up to the proposed sectoral cap.

Source: Government of India (2010).

During this phase of relaxation of FDI policies, an important element was the decision to allow wholly foreign-owned companies through the automatic route in townships, housing, built-up infrastructure and construction-development projects.[7] The year 2005 also witnessed the enactment of the Special Economic Zones (SEZ) Act, which opened further vistas for the involvement of foreign firms in the Indian economy, especially after the modification of the FDI policy in 2006, to permit FDI up to 100 per cent foreign equity (Government of India 2006b). Alongside liberalising the FDI regime, the government declared its intention in 1992 to allow FPI into the Indian stock market through the mechanism of foreign institutional investors.[8] The objective was not only to facilitate non-debt creating foreign capital inflows, but also to develop the stock market in India, lower the cost of capital for Indian enterprises and indirectly improve corporate governance structures. On their part, large Indian companies have been allowed to raise capital directly from international capital markets through commercial borrowings and depository receipts. Thus, the country adopted a two-pronged strategy: one, to attract FDI and, two, to encourage portfolio capital flows to ease the financing constraints of Indian enterprises.

As a result of the aforementioned policy changes, by the early 2000s, India followed an FDI-friendly regime that is quite comparable to that adopted by most countries.[9] One can see the bunching of FDI policy changes applicable to different sectors in at least four years since the year 2000 (Table 4.1). These years are within two years of a government getting a fresh mandate from the people. It may not be a coincidence that in respect of two of these years, the current account deficit (CAD) had increased substantially in the previous financial year. The budget speech of 2013–14 made the objective of meeting the CAD even more explicit.

Much of the foreign investment could take advantage of the automatic approval route without seeking prior permission of the central government. Caps on FDI shareholding began to be applied to only a few sectors, mainly in the services sector.[10]

Table 4.1: Number of Sectors Subjected to FDI Policy Changes, 1997–2016

Year	*No. of Sectors Affected*
1997	2
1998	2
1999	1
2000	29
2001	8
2002	3
2004	4
2005	5
2006	21
2008	9
2009	2
2011	2
2012	16
2013	4
2014	3
2015	7
2016	18
Grand Total	136

Source: Based on a tabulation of FDI policy changes announced through Press Notes and Consolidate FDI Policy documents. Changes in CAD are calculated from the data provided by the RBI on its website.

Concomitant steps were taken to remove the hurdles in the path of foreign investors, both at the stage of entry and later in the process of establishing the venture. The policy changes were thus aimed at improving India's record in attracting FDI inflows, which was seen to be below its potential. As a result of the relaxations effected by successive governments, there remain very few activities where government approval is required and even fewer ones where sectoral caps are applicable (Table 4.2). As a logical next step, the government abolished the FIPB during 2017–18, thus ending the era of scrutinising FDI before it could be invested in India.

Table 4.2: Activities Requiring Central Government Approval or Having Caps

Activity	*Upper Limit for FDI*
A. Government approval with or without caps	
Mining and mineral separation of titanium-bearing minerals and ores	Up to 100%
Defence	Beyond 49% and up to 100%
Publishing/printing of scientific and technical magazines/specialty journals/periodicals	Up to 100%
Publication of facsimile edition of foreign newspapers	Up to 100%
Print media: publishing of newspaper and periodicals dealing with news and current affairs	Up to 26%
Print media: publication of Indian editions of foreign magazines dealing with news and current affairs	Up to 26%
Air transport service: scheduled and regional air transport service	Beyond 49% and up to 100%
Satellites: establishment and operation	Up to 100%
Telecom services	Beyond 49% and up to 100%
Pharma: brownfield	Beyond 74% and up to 100%
Banking: private sector	Beyond 49% and up to 74%
Banking: public sector	Up to 20%
Private security agencies	Beyond 49% and up to 74%
Broadcasting content service	
1. FM radio	Up to 49%
2. Uplinking of 'news and current affairs' TV channels	Up to 49%
Trading: MBRT	Up to 51%
B. Other activities having a cap on FDI	
Insurance	49%
Pension sector	49%
Infrastructure companies in securities markets	49%
Petroleum refining by the public sector undertakings	49%
Power exchanges	49%

Source: Government of India (2017).

The policy debate on FDI has raised two sets of issues: (a) the distinction between direct and portfolio investment; and (b) imposition of foreign investment caps in order to limit the extent of control of the foreign investors over the enterprises they invested in. These issues will be dealt with in this chapter.

Attempt to Differentiate between Direct and Portfolio Investments

We mentioned earlier that the issue of differentiating FDI from portfolio investments arose in the 1990s following the adoption of economic reforms. This was to serve two purposes. One, although the policy of imposing caps on foreign shareholding in the equity of companies was progressively diluted, this policy was was not dispensed with because caps were used on grounds of national security, national sensitivities, sectoral interests and public health, among others. A related issue was whether investments by FIIs should be included while implementing the caps on foreign shareholding.

A second purpose for distinguishing between FDI and FPI is the oft-stated objective of giving preference to long-term FDI over the volatile FPI in view of the large CAD. The then Union finance minister had set the ball rolling in his budget speech of 2013–14 when he said:

> In order to remove the ambiguity that prevails on what is Foreign Direct Investment (FDI) and what is Foreign Institutional Investment (FII), I propose to follow the international practice and lay down a broad principle that, where an investor has a stake of 10 percent or less in a company, it will be treated as FII and, where an investor has a stake of more than 10 percent, it will be treated as FDI. (Government of India 2013: paragraph 95)

Further, the budget speech of 2013–14 stated: '... India, at the present juncture [facing a huge CAD], does not have the choice between welcoming and spurning foreign investment. If I may be frank, foreign investment is an imperative. What we can do is to encourage foreign investment that is consistent with our economic objectives' (ibid.: paragraph 11).

The announcement in the Union budget of 2013–14 was followed by the appointment of the Committee for Rationalising the Definition of FDI and FII, which was headed by the then secretary of the department of economic affairs in March 2013. The committee came to be known as the Mayaram Committee, named after its chairman. The Securities and Exchange Board of India (SEBI) had appointed another committee earlier, in December 2012, headed by a former revenue secretary to study the convergence of the various portfolio investment regimes. One of the recommendations of this committee was in line with the finance minister's statement, as it suggested a cut-off point of 10 per cent for distinguishing the two types of foreign investments. The Mayaram Committee took a long time in finalising its recommendations (Government of India 2014). In its brief report, it re-endorsed the 10 per cent criterion, and its recommendations were concerned with administrative issues only. However, exceptions to the 10 per cent rule suggested by it make identifying an investment as FDI or portfolio investment, without having access to additional information, difficult. Significantly, it differentiated between investments in listed and unlisted companies and supported the prevailing approach of treating all foreign investments in unlisted companies as FDI. The Committee made no attempt to question the basic definition and, hence, provided no guidance for distinguishing FDI and FPI in general.

DIPP, whose role and functions include 'Formulation of Foreign Direct Investment (FDI) Policy and promotion, approval and facilitation of FDI' (Government of India 2018b), raised several questions on the adoption of the 10 per cent rule for measuring FDI:

- a percentage definition does not take note of the qualitative aspect of the more stable nature of FDI;
- change in definition would create complications as the current policy is bound in several bilateral and multilateral agreements; and
- the OECD Benchmark Definition is not followed even by all the OECD member countries (*Economic Times* 2013).

What one can, however, surmise is that the distinction between FDI and FPI and other investors made at the policy level does not extend to the reporting of FDI inflows. As noted in Table 4.2, caps are now applicable to only a few sectors, including banking, insurance, pension, broadcasting (carriage and content) services, print media, power exchanges and multi-brand retail trading (MBRT).[11] In case of private sector banks, the 74 per cent limit includes all forms of foreign investment, namely FIIs/ FPIs, remittances from non-resident Indians (NRIs), erstwhile overseas corporate bodies (OCBs), private placements, global depositary receipts (GDR)/American depositary receipts (ADR) and acquisition of shares from existing shareholders. Had foreign financial investors been treated as a separate category, the story of Flipkart, which was taken over by Walmart in 2018, would probably have been different. On the other hand, the defective categorisation of indirect FDI helped Amazon participate in the inventory model of e-commerce.

The various categories of foreign investors have been defined under respective schedules of the Foreign Exchange Management Act (Transfer or Issue of Securities by Persons Resident Outside India) Regulations 2000. Incidentally, these regulations do not specify any minimum percentage for investments through the FDI route. Since it is not specified that the investee company should have been listed, it follows that the portfolio investors registered with SEBI under relevant categories can directly invest in Indian companies through the automatic route. Thus, such portfolio investments will be reported under the automatic route of FDI for statistical purposes.

As far as the operation of caps on foreign equity is concerned, an important change was introduced relating to indirect equity. Following Press Note No. 2 (Government of India 2009), for measuring indirect foreign equity, further investments by companies with 49 per cent foreign equity and controlled by Indians are treated as domestic investments. Compared to the earlier proportionate method, this is a better way of looking at FDI from the point of caps, as caps are meant to restrict foreign influence/control rather than the economic benefit that is derived by the foreign investor. However, it is debatable if any foreign investor contributing up to 49 per cent risk capital would be content to remain a sleeping partner. In fact, the discussion paper of DIPP on FDI caps 'implicitly recognises that foreign equity, up to 49%, is purely a source of funding, as long as "control" is not yielded to non-resident investors/entities' (Government of India 2011: paragraph 21).

Given the fact that there is effectively no explicit restriction on the extent of foreign control at the point of entry, the subsequent efforts at limiting control through monitoring indirect foreign equity would be of little consequence. Since retaining some control in Indian hands appears to be the main objective of applying caps, the following points may be in order. It would be unrealistic to expect that foreign investors would not be interested in securing their technology and reputation, besides maximising their overall gains. This is especially due to the fact that the joint venture came into being mainly because of the restrictive FDI regime, in the absence of which they would most probably have opted for a wholly owned venture. On the other hand, the Indian partner would go for an FDI relationship, mainly to derive substantial advantages in terms of technology, goodwill, etc., apart from obtaining a stable risk capital. This is likely to place them at a disadvantage in negotiating with the foreign partner, thus making them more likely to concede control of the operations and strategy to the foreign investor. The subordinate relationship would be covered up only to meet the requirements of the official policy on FDI, which places limits on foreign participation, on paper. The disproportionate control of the boards conceded to the foreign partners in the joint ventures of the insurance and defence industries clearly points to this phenomenon. Further, without any criteria on the nature of the domestic partner, the objective of the cap could be defeated.[12] These reflect the policymakers' dilemma to maintain caps on foreign shareholding while also trying to attract inflows.

In sum, Indian policymakers never really took into consideration corporate control mechanisms for adopting FDI policies. Evidently, in the post-1991 period, the caps were deployed mechanically. Besides, there was inconsistency in treating financial investors in the FDI policy. Using FDI to finance CAD on the one hand, and infrastructure like housing on the other, undermined the main justification for seeking this form of capital emphasised by the Statement of Industrial Policy of 1991, namely that it would bring with it technology, management skills and other intangibles. While the international thumb rule of 10 per cent for identifying an FDI relationship fails to distinguish between investment that brings with it the intangibles like technology and advanced management techniques, India's approach, which did not consider even this thumb rule, has further obliterated the distinction between direct and portfolio investments.

Notes

1. Several sectors, like IT, were opened up to foreign investment after the mid-1980s. For details, see Dhar and Joseph (2019: 98, 104).

2. See Nehru's statement in Parliament on 6 April 1949. Before that, in the IPS of 6 April 1948, the policy regarding the participation of foreign capital was mentioned in very broad terms (India 1948: 2385–86).

3. An institution with similar functions, namely the FIPB, was established in 1991 to expedite approval of foreign investment proposals.

4. It was an Act to consolidate and amend the law regulating certain payments, dealing in foreign exchange and securities, transactions indirectly affecting foreign exchange, and the import and export of currency, for the conservation of the foreign exchange resources of the country and the proper utilisation thereof in the interest of the economic development of the country.

5. The return of Indira Gandhi to power in 1980 marked the beginning of the process of relaxation of the regulations.

6. The distinction had to be made probably because the government decided to allow FPI in the stock market.

7. This includes, but is not restricted to, housing, commercial premises, hotels, resorts, hospitals, educational institutions, recreational facilities, and city- and regional-level infrastructure, subject to certain guidelines.

8. 'We will also consider ways of allowing reputable foreign investors, such as pension funds, to invest in our capital markets, with suitable mechanisms to ensure that this does not threaten loss of management control' (Government of India 1992a).

9. See Planning Commission (2002) and IMF (2005).

10. These included air-transport services, rail infrastructure, insurance and pension sectors, defence sector, broadcasting sector, banking (private sector), power exchanges, brownfield pharmaceuticals and private security agencies. Besides, FDI is not permitted in a few areas like agriculture (except floriculture, horticulture, development of seeds, animal husbandry, pisciculture, aquaculture and cultivation of

vegetables and mushrooms), retail trading (except single-brand product retailing), lottery, gambling and betting, chit fund, mutual-benefit financial companies, trading in transferable development rights, real estate, manufacturing of cigars, cigarettes, tobacco or tobacco substitutes, atomic energy, and railway transport (other than mass rapid transport systems). See Government of India (2017, 2018).

11. In some activities, though there was a sub-limit for automatic entry, FDI could go up to 100 per cent with government approval.

12. For instance, Amazon exploited this loophole by partnering with a domestic private equity firm that has no (long- or short-term direct) interest in retail trade (Rai 2014).

References

'Reforms Get Stuck in FDI *versus* FII Fight as DIPP Opposes Change in Definition of FDI'. 2013. *Economic Times*, 8 May. Available at https://economictimes.indiatimes.com/news/economy/policy/reforms-get-stuck-in-fdi-versus-fii-fight-as-dipp-opposes-change-in-definition-of-fdi/articleshow/19939688.cms (accessed 18 July 2018).

BM. 1984. 'Luring Multinationals into High Technology Areas'. *Economic and Political Weekly* 19 (14), 7 April: 585–86.

Chaudhuri, Sudip. 1979. 'FERA: Appearance and Reality'. *Economic and Political Weekly* 14 (16), 21 April: 734–44.

Dhar, Biswajit. 1988. 'State Regulation of Foreign Capital in India'. Working paper no. 6, Institute for Studies in Industrial Development. Available at http://isid.org.in/pdf/statreg.PDF (accessed 18 July 2018).

Dhar, Biswajit and Reji K. Joseph. 2019. 'India's Information Technology Industry: A Tale of Two Halves'. In *Innovation, Economic Development, and Intellectual Property in India and China*, eds Kung-Chung Liu and Uday S. Racherla, 93–117. Singapore: Springer Open. Available at https://link.springer.com/content/pdf/10.1007%2F978-981-13-8102-7.pdf (accessed 30 January 2020).

Dhar, Biswajit, Reji Joseph and T. C. James. 2012. 'India's Bilateral Investment Agreements: Time to Review'. *Economic and Political Weekly* 47 (52), 29 December: 113–22.

Ganesan, A. V. 1982. 'Domestic Participation in Ownership of Existing Transnational Corporation Subsidiaries in Developing Countries: The Indian Experience'. Workshop on Regulating and Negotiating with Transnational Corporations, Port of Spain, 5–18 July.

Government of India. 1967. 'Report of the Committee on Foreign Collaboration' (Chairman: Mr A. Ramaswami Mudaliar). Ministry of Industrial Development and Company Affairs, New Delhi.

———. 1991a. 'Budget 1991–92: Speech of Shri Manmohan Singh, Minister of Finance'. Available at https://www.indiabudget.gov.in/doc/bspeech/bs199192.pdf (accessed 20 July 2018).

———. 1991b. 'Statement on Industrial Policy'. Department for Promotion of Industry and Internal Trade, 24 July. Available at https://dipp.gov.in/sites/default/files/chap001_0_0.pdf (accessed 25 July 2018).

———. 1992a. 'Budget 1992–93: Speech of Shri Manmohan Singh, Minister of Finance'. Available at https://dea.gov.in/sites/default/files/Union%20Budget%201992-93.pdf (accessed 20 July 2018).

———. 1992b. 'Press Note No. 12 (1992 Series): Withdrawal of the Condition Regarding "Dividend Balancing"'. Available at https://dipp.gov.in/sites/default/files/chap005_0.pdf (accessed 25 July 2018).

———. 1993. 'Budget 1993–94: Speech of Shri Manmohan Singh, Minister of Finance'. Available at https://www.indiabudget.gov.in/doc/bspeech/bs199394.pdf (accessed 20 July 2018).

———. 1996. 'Press Note No. 4 (1996 Series): Further Liberalisation in Parameters for Automatic Approval in Foreign Collaboration'. Available at https://dipp.gov.in/sites/default/files/chap007_0.pdf (accessed 25 July 2018).

———. 2000a. 'Press Note No. 7 (2000 Series): Review of Existing Sectoral Policy and Sectoral Equity Cap for Foreign Direct Investment (FDI) / Non-resident Indian (NRI) / Overseas Corporate Bodies (OCB) Investment'. Available at https://dipp.gov.in/sites/default/files/pn28.pdf (accessed 25 July 2018).

Government of India. 2000b. 'Press Note No. 10 (2000 Series): Review of Existing Sectoral Policy and Sectoral Equity Cap for Foreign Direct Investment (FDI) and Investment by Non-resident Indians (NRI) / Overseas Corporate Bodies (OCB)'. Available at https://dipp.gov.in/sites/default/files/pn31.pdf (accessed 25 July 2018).

_____. 2001. 'Press Note No. 4 (2001 Series): Revision of Existing Sectoral Guidelines and Equity Cap on Foreign Direct Investment (FDI), Including Investment by Non-resident Indians (NRIs) and Overseas Corporate Bodies (OCBs)'.Available at https://dipp.gov.in/sites/default/files/pn44.pdf (accessed 25 July 2018).

_____. 2002. 'Press Note No. 2 (2002 Series): Guidelines for Licensing Production of Arms and Ammunitions'. Available at https://dipp.gov.in/sites/default/files/pn52.pdf (accessed 25 July 2018).

_____. 2006a. 'Press Note No. 3 (2006 Series): Guidelines for FDI in Retail Trade of "Single Brand" Products'. Available at https://dipp.gov.in/sites/default/files/pn3_2006_0.pdf (accessed 25 July 2018).

_____. 2006b. Press Note No. 4 (2006 Series): Rationalisation of the FDI Policy'. Available at https://dipp.gov.in/sites/default/files/pn4_2006_0.pdf (accessed 25 July 2018).

_____. 2009. 'Press Note No. 2 (2009 Series): Guidelines for Calculation of Total Foreign Investment, i.e. Direct and Indirect Foreign Investment in Indian Companies'. Available at https://dipp.gov.in/sites/default/files/pn2_2009_1.pdf (accessed 25 July 2018).

_____. 2010. 'Foreign Direct Investment (FDI) in Defence Sector'. Department of Industrial Policy and Promotion. Available at https://dipp.gov.in/sites/default/files/DiscussionPapers_17May2010%20%204.pdf (accessed 25 July 2018).

_____. 2011. 'Discussion Paper: FDI Policy-Rationale and Relevance of Caps'. Available at https://dipp.gov.in/sites/default/files/DiscussionPaper_relevance_23June2011%20%205.pdf (accessed 25 July 2018).

_____. 2013. 'Budget 2013–2014: Speech of P. Chidambaram, Minister of Finance'. Available at https://www.indiabudget.gov.in/budget2013-2014/ub2013-14/bs/bs.pdf (accessed 20 July 2018).

Government of India. 2014. 'Report of the Dr Arvind Mayaram Committee on Rationalizing the FDI/FII Definition'. Ministry of Finance, Department of Economic Affairs, June. Available at https://www.finmin.nic.in/sites/default/files/Report%20of%20Dr%20Arvind%20Mayaram%20committe%20on%20FDI_FII.pdf (accessed 20 July 2018).

______. 2017. 'Consolidated FDI Policy (Effective from August 28, 2017)'. Department of Industrial Policy and Promotion, Ministry of Commerce and Industry. Available at http://dipp.nic.in/policies-rules-and-acts/policies/foreign-direct-investment-policy (accessed 25 July 2018).

______. 2018a. 'India: The World's Most Open Economy for FDI, Multiple New Sectors Opened up for FDI'. *Make in India*. Available at http://www.makeinindia.com/article/-/v/india-is-now-the-most-open-economy-in-the-world-for-fdi (accessed 30 July 2018).

______. 2018b. 'Role and Functions of the Department for Promotion of Industry and Internal Trade'. Department for Promotion of Industry and Internal Trade. Available at https://dipp.gov.in/about-us/role-and-functions-department-promotion-industry-and-internal-trade (accessed 31 July 2018).

IMF. 2005. 'Foreign Direct Investment in India: How Can it be Increased?'. *India: Selected Issues*, 7 January. Available at http://www.imf.org/external/pubs/ft/scr/2005/cr0587.pdf (accessed 5 July 2018).

India. 1948. 'Constituent Assembly of India (Legislative) Debates, Vol. III, No. 1', 2385–86.

Joshi, Vijay and I. M. D. Little. 1996. *India's Economic Reforms, 1991–2001*. Oxford: Clarendon Press.

Kidron, Michael.1965. *Foreign Investments in India*. London: Oxford University Press.

Kust, Matthew J. 1964. *Foreign Enterprise in India: Laws and Policies*. Chapel Hill, North Carolina: University of North Carolina Press.

Martinussen, John. 1988. *Transnational Corporations in a Developing Country: The Indian Experience*. New Delhi: Sage Publications.

Planning Commission. 2002. 'Report of the Steering Group on Foreign Direct Investment'. August, 22.

Rai, Saritha. 2014. 'Amazon Ties Up with IT Billionaire Murthy of Infosys to Launch e-Commerce Joint Venture in India'. *Forbes*, 27 June. Available at https://www.forbes.com/sites/saritharai/2014/06/27/amazon-ties-up-with-it-billionaire-murthy-of-infosys-to-launch-e-commerce-joint-venture-in-india/#74b7ef04f7a6 (accessed 5 July 2018).

US Department of Commerce. 1963. 'Investment in India: Conditions and Outlook for United States Investors'. Washington, D. C.

five

India's FDI Inflows since 1991

This chapter analyses the trends in and the underlying features of FDI inflows into India since 1991, the period in which Government of India progressively removed almost all restrictions on foreign investors. We will use the available official data on the participation of FDI in India since 1991 to help understand the changing nature of FDI since the adoption of the economic reforms programme. Before we get into the numbers describing the nature of FDI participation, we will provide a brief snapshot of the database on FDI statistics. This is vital for understanding the quality of official data, and of course, the nature of conclusions that can be made about FDI in India.

Understanding the Database on FDI in India

The RBI and DPIIT, Ministry of Commerce and Industry, provide data on FDI. The latter is the 'nodal Department for formulation of the policy of the Government on Foreign Direct Investment (FDI)' (DPIIT 2019) and, as part of the erstwhile FIPB, has also been responsible for screening FDI proposals.[1] The DPIIT 'is also responsible for maintenance and management of data on inward FDI into India, based upon the remittances reported by the Reserve Bank of India' (ibid.). However, despite this apparent synergy between the RBI and DPIIT, the data presented by each agency is on occasion not comparable, which we shall enumerate briefly.

First, let us consider the availability of data on FDI inflows. The RBI has provided data on inflows for each financial year beginning 1990–91. From 1991–92, RBI data has informed on the magnitude of investments 'routed' through the FIPB, after receiving government approvals, or entering through the 'automatic route'. Another important aspect of the FDI data is that until 1994–95, data on 'acquisition of shares' by foreign companies, or cases of M&A, were not reported.[2]

Yet another limitation of RBI data, one which runs right through the post-1991 period, is that this institution does not provide a comprehensive set of disaggregated data in terms of either the source countries of FDI or the sectors in which such investments are made. Although a partially disaggregated set of data is provided in the RBI's annual report of 2010–11, covering the period from 2006–07, the available data does not give the full flavour of the nature of FDI inflows.

The DPIIT has addressed this limitation to a considerable extent by providing data for sources of FDI inflows and their sectoral distribution from 1996. The Secretariat for Industrial Approvals, now renamed Secretariat for Industrial Assistance (SIA), provided disaggregated data from 1991 until the early years of the following decade. However, this database provided information, not on the actual FDI inflows, but on approvals granted by the government to the proposals of foreign investors. This data had three limitations. First, since figures for proposed foreign investments and not actual FDI inflows were reported, it was not possible to decipher from this database the proportion of the approvals which eventually fructified. A second lacuna was that the database did not allow us to identify the number of foreign investment projects in which the foreign investors had effective control. This lacuna was felt because the agencies engaged in regulating the entry of foreign capital did not distinguish between the analytically distinct categories of direct and portfolio investments. These agencies were only providing information on the proposed financial collaborations, or on projects in which the foreign investors were intending to make investments in foreign currency. A third, and a relatively minor issue, was that the DPIIT provided the disaggregated data for calendar years, as opposed to financial years, the period used for reporting the later data.

The lack of a clear distinction between FDI and FPI is, in our view, the most serious limitation of the official data on FDI inflows. In addition to the conceptual point made in Chapter 4, there are at least two contributory factors, both arising from the lack of clarity in defining the components of FDI in official statistics. The first is that from 1994, data on approvals of FDI into India included GDRs/ADRs, and foreign currency convertible bonds (FCCBs) and external commercial borrowings (ECBs). These forms of inflows are, in effect, portfolio investments/borrowings, essentially because they lack the key characteristics of direct investment, namely control of the foreign investor over the invested company. Counting these inflows as FDI is, therefore, erroneous.

Overstatement of FDI inflows stemming from the inclusion of GDRs/ADRs becomes obvious if the official data is closely examined. GDRs were first included in FDI approvals in 1994, adding Rs 52 billion ($1.6 billion) to the total approvals and increasing them by 60 per cent as compared to the figure for 1993 (Government of India 1995: 4). Had the GDRs not been included, approved FDI for 1994 would have been marginally higher than the approved FDI for 1993.

The next issue is regarding the comparability of FDI data provided by the RBI and subsequently reported by the DPIIT. We discussed in Chapter 4 that until the end of the 1990s, the composition of FDI was quite different from that of the present. For instance, retained earnings were excluded from FDI statistics (RBI 2010: 2). In this period, FDI inflows to and from India comprised mainly of equity capital. India adopted the international best practices given by IMF's BPM5, on recommendation of the Technical Monitoring Group (TMG) on FDI statistics (ibid.: 83). The coverage of FDI was, thus, expanded from 2000–01 to include equity capital, reinvested earnings (or retained earnings of FDI companies) and 'other direct capital' (inter-corporate debt transactions between related entities) (RBI 2007: 223). Clarifying what 'other capital' comprises, RBI stated that this 'part of FDI inflow has been carved out from the figure reported under external commercial borrowings' (ibid.). But, as discussed earlier, the RBI had previously noted that ECBs were no more than portfolio investments. However, in its revised format for presenting the data on foreign investment, GDRs and ADRs were excluded from FDI, while other ECBs were included. There are, therefore, considerable problems with India's data on FDI, especially their comparability with those from countries that strictly adhere to the OECD/IMF Benchmark Definitions.

It can be concluded from the foregoing discussion that the official agencies in India have not followed the definition given by OECD/IMF that helps in distinguishing between FDI inflows and those that are not, using the criteria of 10 per cent of voting shares. Interestingly, the RBI admits to this lacuna when it states that the 'present definition being used to classify FDI in India is at variance with this definition (to the extent that the threshold limit of 10% is not strictly adhered to)' (RBI 2010: 10). This is a significant statement as it lays bare the problems with India's FDI data, namely that the distinction between direct and portfolio investments is, at best, fuzzy. In the ensuing paragraphs, we shall try to explain this hiatus between the OECD/IMF definition of

FDI and that adopted by the Indian agencies. Our view is that the nature of the administrative mechanisms that have been in place for regulating the entry of foreign investors into India are responsible for creating this hiatus

From the early post-Independence years, Government of India encouraged foreign companies to enter through joint ventures, commonly called foreign collaborations. This was the message of the policy note issued in 1961 on the role of foreign capital in India's industrialisation (Kust 1964: 142). Foreign collaboration approvals were essentially of two types. One, foreign companies contributed only technology ('technical collaborations') and other know-how to unaffiliated enterprises, and two, foreign investors made capital infusion into enterprises, both affiliated and unaffiliated ('financial collaborations'). The latter could be done either in association with Indian partners or through sole ventures.

We discussed in Chapter 4 that the Statement of Industrial Policy of July 1991 set in motion the process of progressively exempting foreign investors from mandatory government approvals. Initially, 'automatic approvals' were made applicable to foreign investors investing up to 51 per cent foreign equity in an enterprise belonging to a set of identified high-priority industries. The upper limit of foreign shareholding in cases of 'automatic approval' was raised in 1997 from 51 per cent to 74 per cent (100 per cent in case of investments by NRIs) in notified industries. Over the next two decades, FDI policy underwent two important modifications. First, the ambit of government approval was drastically reduced and, second, caps on foreign shareholding were progressively raised and eventually eliminated in most sectors. As discussed in Chapter 4, this meant that automatic approval was expanded to cover almost the entire manufacturing sector, and several activities in the agricultural and the services sectors as well. Government approvals currently cover only a small set of sectors.

Finally, a comment on DIPP's reporting of sectoral and source-wise inflows of FDI, which, in our view, has yet another conceptual ambiguity. The agency has all along reported intra- and inter-corporate inflows of capital, which implies that the inflows should include both equity capital and 'other capital', following the OECD/IMF definition. Until the Indian agencies took steps towards adopting international norms for reporting FDI data, there was no compulsion to report 'other capital' in the statistics. However, even after 2000–01, there was a need to clarify whether FDI inflows included only equity capital or 'other capital' as well. Not only was this clarification not provided, DPIIT used the term 'FDI Equity Inflows' for reporting data from 2012–13. Given that DPIIT has not clarified the nature of inflows prior to 2012–13 and also that much of the approvals data made available for the 1990s did not include 'other capital', we would use the term 'FDI equity' when we use the DPIIT database for analysing the sectoral behaviour of inflows and the countries contributing to these inflows.

Considering the foregoing discussion, three comments about the quality of FDI data provided by the government agencies are in order. First, data on FDI from 1991–92 to 1999–2000 cannot be compared with the data either from the earlier or the subsequent decades. Second, agencies providing the FDI data have not ensured that the data is consistent over time. This problem is acutely felt when the data is disaggregated in terms of the sectors or the providing countries. Third, India's FDI data is not comparable with that of other countries, since the RBI does not 'strictly' adhere to criteria for identifying FDI provided by the OECD/IMF while computing the data.

In the following sections, we will discuss the features and trends in FDI inflows since 1991. It covers three periods: the decade of the 1990s; the first decade of the new millennium; and

2010–11 to 2017–18. While this periodisation can be justified on the grounds of the availability of comparable datasets, it is also dictated by both the quality of data and quantity of foreign investment flows. It may be recalled that the data for the first period is available only for the approved cases of FDI. In the second period, Indian agencies took steps towards adopting the global best practice in reporting statistics on FDI, developed by the OECD and IMF, and therefore, the datasets are more comparable. The third period marks the quantum jump in FDI inflows following the unshackling of foreign investors investing in India.

Foreign Investment Inflows in the First Decade of Economic Reforms

In this section, we will try to quantify the impact of the Indian government's favourable regime by providing estimates of foreign investment inflows. Table 5.1 provides the broad trends in FDI inflows in the 1990s.

Foreign investors responded positively to the easing of controls over their operations, ushered in by the economic reforms programme. Immediately preceding economic reforms, inflows of FDI were less than $100 million, and as Table 5.1 shows, there was a steady increase in inflows thereafter. Between 1991–92 and 1994–95, FDI inflows increased more than 10-fold. This evidence of positive response of FDI to the policy changes effected in 1991 strengthens if the FDI data for the late 1980s is also considered. This data requires some adjustments since data for actual inflows of FDI is not available; data on FDI approvals is provided by the official agencies. In 1989, the year that witnessed the peaking of FDI inflows for the entire decade, the total FDI inflows did not

Table 5.1: FDI Inflows into India, 1991–2000 ($ Million)

Years	*Direct Investment to India*	*Equity*	*Government (SIA/FIPB)*	*RBI*	*NRI*	*Acquisition of Shares*
1990–91	97	—	—	—	—	—
1991–92	129	129	66	—	63	—
1992–93	315	315	222	42	51	—
1993–94	586	586	280	89	217	—
1994–95	1,314	1,314	701	171	442	—
1995–96	2,144	2,144	1,249	169	715	11
1996–97	2,821	2,821	1,922	135	639	125
1997–98	3,557	3,557	2,754	202	241	360
1998–99	2,462	2,462	1,821	179	62	400
1999–2000	2,155	2,155	1,410	171	84	490

Source: *Database of the Indian Economy*, 2018, RBI, available at https://dbie.rbi.org.in/DBIE/dbie.rbi?site=statistics (accessed 5 August 2018).

cross the threshold of 50 million,[3] which was almost half of the inflows in 1990–91. It should be noted that the increase in inflows during 1990–91 took place despite the critical balance of payments situation (Institute for Studies in Industrial Development 1995).[4]

Significant increases in FDI inflows occurred from 1995, when inflows touched the $2 billion mark. The increase in inflows seems more impressive considering that the rupee had depreciated by more than 40 per cent during this period. In other words, FDI had the potential of contributing more to the capital formation of the country in terms of the domestic currency.

The inflow figures after the mid-1990s were reported separately for the acquisition of shares by foreign companies or M&As. M&A activities, first reported in 1995–96, were quite modest, but by the end of the decade, they had increased to more than 22 per cent of the total inflows.

Industry-wise Pattern of Approvals

We discussed in Chapter 4 that the primary objective of the reform of the FDI policy framework undertaken by the government was to provide incentives to foreign investors to participate in high-technology and export-intensive sectors.

This was emphasised in the Statement of Industrial Policy, which said: 'foreign investment and technology collaboration will be welcomed to obtain higher technology, to increase exports and to expand the production base' (Government of India 1991: paragraph 13).

The focus of the FDI policies was on attracting investments for stimulating India's industrial sector, and the data on FDI approvals in terms of the value of foreign investments shows that the industrial sector had an overwhelmingly large share of the cases involving approvals of FDI.[5] Except in 1996, when the share of the services sector in the approved investments was more than 18 per cent, the industrial sector had a share well above 85 per cent of the approved FDI cases during 1991–2000. It may, however, be pointed out that this trend was along expected lines, since most of the services sectors (and agriculture) were not open for foreign investors to the extent that the industrial sector was.

Table 5.2 gives the details of FDI approvals in terms of value for the top-10 sectors during 1991–2000. These sectors explain a large share of the approvals: 80 per cent for the entire period, and 95 per cent in the year 2000.

Before we dwell on the sectoral composition of approvals, we should remember that the data presented in Tables 5.1 and 5.2 includes not only the approvals for FDI, but also for portfolio investment in the form of ADRs, GDRs and other forms of non-FDI inflows.

Table 5.2: FDI Approvals by Major Sectors, 1991–2000 ($ Million)

Sectors	*1991–95*	*1996*	*1997*	*1998*	*1999*	*2000*	*1991–2000*
Fuels (power and oil refinery)	4,093.1 (19.7)	1,623.5 (15.9)	7,279.0 (48.2)	3,366.9 (45.1)	1,317.7 (20.0)	1,282.9 (15.6)	18,963.3 (27.7)
Telecommunications	6,302.3 (30.3)	1,252.0 (12.3)	1,978.8 (13.1)	751.4 (10.1)	906.2 (13.8)	2,056.4 (25.0)	13,247.1 (19.4)
Electrical equipment (including computer software)	969.9 (4.7)	881.1 (8.6)	603.9 (4.0)	346.0 (4.6)	592.2 (9.0)	2,784.4 (33.8)	6,177.6 (9.0)
Transportation industry	1,040.4 (5.0)	812.5 (8.0)	1,043.7 (6.9)	378.8 (5.1)	1,444.8 (21.9)	226.8 (2.8)	4,947.1 (7.2)
Services sector	1,107.3 (5.3)	1,487.2 (14.6)	395.7 (2.6)	411.3 (5.5)	531.4 (8.1)	307.4 (3.7)	4,240.3 (6.2)
Metallurgical industry	1,432.9 (6.9)	653.7 (6.4)	693.1 (4.6)	538.0 (7.2)	325.2 (4.9)	407.2 (4.9)	4,050.1 (5.9)
Chemical (other than fertilisers)	1,244.9 (6.0)	855.1 (8.4)	778.6 (5.2)	440 (5.9)	188.2 (2.9)	58.1 (0.7)	3,564.5 (5.0)
Food-processing industries	838.2 (4.0)	955.3 (9.4)	530.6 (3.5)	153.3 (2.1)	32.8 (0.5)	61.3 (0.7)	2,571.5 (3.5)
Hotel and tourism	641.1 (3.1)	126.7 (1.2)	200.5 (1.3)	116.5 (1.6)	182.2 (2.8)	83.4 (1.0)	1,350.4 (2.0)
Miscellaneous industries	392.6 (1.9)	231.9 (2.3)	88.5 (0.6)	53.7 (0.7)	199.2 (3.0)	174.5 (2.1)	1,140.4 (1.7)
Total for the top-10 sectors	16,168.0 (77.6)	7,182.7 (70.4)	12,366.5 (81.8)	6,150.7 (82.4)	5,572.8 (84.6)	7,837.4 (95.1)	55,278.1 (77.0)
Total FDI approvals	20,824.8	10,201.4	15,116.1	7,468.2	6,588.4	8,241.7	71,752.3

Note: Figures in parentheses are percentage shares of the total approvals for the year/period.

Source: *Handbook of Industrial Policy and Statistics*, 2001, Ministry of Commerce and Industry, Government of India.

The top-three sectors in terms of the combined FDI approvals for 1991–2000, namely electrical equipment, telecommunications and fuels, accounted for 56 per cent of all proposed investments. The dilution of the post-Independence industrial policy during the 1990s, leading to the dereservation of areas earlier reserved for public sector enterprises,[6] was a possible trigger for the dramatic rise in FDI approvals in these sectors. The iron and steel, and transportation industries were the two sectors in which this shift in policy allowed foreign companies to look for investment opportunities, the evidence of which is in Table 5.2. The automobile industry was among the industries in which consolidation of foreign companies during the 1990s changed the character of industry. The pharmaceutical industry is another interesting case. Though not on the top-10 list in Table 5.2, this sector, which also had critical presence of the public sector before 1991, due to the changed priorities of the government, saw an increase in interest by foreign companies towards the close of the 1990s.

One of the leading sectors in the list of top-10 sectors was the 'services sector', including banking and other financial services like insurance and non-financial services, like hospital and diagnostic services. During the 1990s, FDI approvals granted to the 'services sector' were mostly for the financial services (nearly 70 per cent of approvals).

Sources of FDI Approvals

Sources from which India received investment proposals were considerably diverse, both in terms of the numbers and the regions. One less-known feature of FDI inflows into India is that many countries are reported to have shown interest in investing in the country. DPIIT reports that during the 1990s, FDI approvals were granted to entities from 94 countries, although the approvals granted were mostly from the top-10 countries (Table 5.3). These countries accounted for more than 75 per cent of the approved investment during 1999–2000.

Countries from which foreign direct investors showed interest in investing in India in the country's early post-reforms phase were mostly industrialised countries. More than three-fourths of the total approvals for FDI came from these countries. The US had a strong presence, with a share of more than 25 per cent in terms of the investments approved during 1991–2000, though its position had become relatively weak in the second half of the 1990s with the emergence of Mauritius as a source country. Mauritius was the second largest potential source of FDI, a position that it would consolidate in the following decades.

Four of the countries listed in Table 5.3 have a common feature: they are recognised as tax havens. Two of these are better known, namely Mauritius and the Netherlands, while two others, South Korea and Malaysia, have also been identified as jurisdictions whose tax regimes have been questioned for lack of necessary transparency (Akhtar and Grondona 2019). Just outside the top-10 list was Singapore, another tax haven which played a significant role as a source of FDI in the subsequent decades.

The final aspect of our discussion in this section concerns an estimation of FDI approvals fructifying into actual investments. In India and elsewhere, governments and foreign companies routinely make announcements about investment projects, but whether these announcements result in actual investments is not widely discussed. While detailed examination of investment data at individual company-level can give some indication about the gaps between the interest shown by a company to invest and the fructification of this investment, there is a data gap at the macro level that prevents examination of this phenomenon. The data on FDI provided by DPIIT for the 1990s allows us to estimate the gaps between approved and actual investments (Table 5.4).

According to Table 5.4, overall, just about a fourth of the total FDI approvals fructified as investments, which may reflect the difficult approval processes existing in India requiring the involvement of a multitude of agencies. The share of actual inflows

Table 5.3: Approved FDI by Top-10 Sources, 1991–2000 ($ Million)

Countries	*1991–95*	*1996*	*1997*	*1998*	*1999*	*2000*	*1991–2000*
US	5,393.9 (30.6)	2,838.0 (35.0)	3,736.9 (27.9)	863.3 (13.3)	830.4 (14.5)	933.4 (26.9)	14,647.0 (25.9)
Mauritius	863.0 (4.9)	658.7 (8.1)	2,871.6 (21.5)	767.3 (11.8)	883.3 (15.4)	1,609.6 (46.3)	8,557.0 (15.1)
UK	1,328.2 (7.5)	430.3 (5.3)	1,236.7 (9.2)	775.8 (11.9)	688.2 (12.0)	91.5 (2.6)	4,764.5 (8.4)
Japan	991.8 (5.6)	420.0 (5.2)	525.0 (3.9)	310.9 (4.8)	370.4 (6.5)	184.1 (5.3)	2,888.5 (5.1)
South Korea	173.5 (1.0)	909.0 (11.2)	538.6 (4.0)	89.3 (1.4)	847.5 (14.8)	9.1 (0.3)	2,829.2 (5.0)
Germany	774.0 (4.4)	434.0 (5.4)	593.7 (4.4)	206.9 (3.2)	265.5 (4.6)	132.1 (3.8)	2,470.4 (4.4)
Australia	700.4 (4.0)	235.5 (2.9)	118.9 (0.9)	639.3 (9.8)	150.7 (2.6)	13.7 (0.4)	1,923.8 (3.4)
Malaysia	522.7 (3.0)	11.9 (0.1)	579.6 (4.3)	437.0 (6.7)	27.0 (0.5)	3.5 (0.1)	1,621.3 (2.9)
France	240.7 (1.4)	471.8 (5.8)	196.5 (1.5)	124.5 (1.9)	336.5 (5.9)	45.0 (1.3)	1,522.7 (2.7)
Netherlands	576.3 (3.3)	296.0 (3.7)	239.7 (1.8)	120.3 (1.8)	146.8 (2.6)	1.0 (0.03)	1,366.4 2.4
Total for top-10 countries	11,564.4 (65.6)	6,705.2 (82.8)	10,637.1 (79.5)	4,334.6 (66.6)	4,546.2 (79.3)	3,023.2 (87.0)	42,590.7 (75.2)
I. Total of all countries	17,634.0	8,097.6	13,375.8	6,505.0	5,733.4	3,475.3	56,642.1
II. NRI	945.3	618.3	500.4	181.9	105.6	360.2	2,772.0
III. Euro-issue GDR/FCCB	2,245.4	1,485.6	1,239.8	781.4	749.3	4,406.3	12,338.3
Total FDI (I + II + III)	20,824.8	10,201.4	15,116.1	7,468.2	6,588.4	8,241.7	71,752.3

Note: Figures in parentheses are percentage shares of the annual approvals.

Source: *Handbook of Industrial Policy and Statistics*, 2001, Ministry of Commerce and Industry, Government of India.

was particularly low in certain sectors—fuels, telecommunications and metallurgical industries. This was either due to the nature of the foreign investors, or the sectoral policy was slow to evolve in areas earlier reserved for the public sector.[7]

Table 5.4: Potential and Actual FDI, 1991–2000 ($ Million)

Years	*Approved FDI*	*Actual Inflows*	*Share of Actual to Approved (%)*
1991–95	20,824.8	3,915.9	18.8
1996	10,201.4	2,467.8	24.2
1997	15,116.1	3,577.0	23.7
1998	7,468.2	3,216.0	43.1
1999	6,588.4	2,150.7	32.6
2000	8,241.7	2,323.3	28.2
1991–2000	68,440.5	17,650.7	25.8

Source: *SIA Newsletter*, DPIIT, various issues.

Analysis of Inflows in the First Decade of the Millennium

The first decade of the millennium was the period in which India's FDI policy was rapidly liberalised. We discussed in Chapter 4 that between 2000 and 2009, FDI policies were amended more than 80 times, covering all the major sectors—agriculture, manufacturing and the services sectors. Another important development was that reporting of FDI data was made compatible with IMF's BPM5.[8] The change in the reporting practice introduced new items, especially reinvested earnings of the already-established enterprises.

Table 5.5 presents the inflows data for the decade 2000–01 to 2009–10. As compared to the earlier methodology, the new approach resulted in a sizeable increase in reported FDI inflows: from $4 billion in 2000–01, FDI inflows increased to nearly $10 billion in 2005–06. Inflows gathered momentum in the second half of the decade, peaking to nearly $42 billion in 2008–09. Thus, FDI inflows grew at an average rate of 15 per cent during 2000–01 to 2004–05 and by nearly 52 per cent in the second half of the decade. The dramatic rise in FDI inflows after 2005–06 resulted from exceptionally high increases in equity inflows (Table 5.5).

Table 5.5: Reported FDI Inflows into India, 2000–10 ($ Million)

Years	*Direct Investment to India*
2000–01	4.0
2001–02	6.1
2002–03	5.0
2003–04	4.3
2004–05	6.1
2005–06	9.7
2006–07	22.8
2007–08	34.8
2008–09	41.9
2009–10	37.7

Source: Based on 'Fact Sheet on Foreign Direct Investment (FDI)', DPIIT, December 2009 and November 2010.

FDI equity inflows during 2005–06 to 2009–10 were almost seven times higher than those in the immediately preceding quinquennium. This trend points to a discernible relationship between the increase in inflows and the extensive relaxation of controls on foreign investors. Caps on the shareholding by foreign investors in enterprises were either raised or removed for several critical sectors, including telecommunications, petroleum (both in exploration and refining) and pharmaceuticals. While in many sectors, foreign investors could hold majority stake, and thereby establish subsidiaries in India, there were several other sectors in which they could fully own enterprises. Alongside, foreign investors were increasingly freed from the approval processes of the government; in other words, funds could be brought into the country directly, through the so-called 'automatic route'.

There is a sub-text to the narrative on India's open-door policy towards FDI, which is that foreign investors did not respond immediately to the policy reforms introduced in the 1990s or even in the early years of the new millennium. The response from foreign investors came with a lag; only after 2005–06 did the inflows increase substantially.

Figure 5.1 captures the steep increase in FDI inflows between 1991 and the end of the 2000s. FDI inflows grew from an annual average of less than $2 billion in the first decade of the economic reforms to over $17.2 billion in the 2000s. Particularly remarkable was the expansion in the inflows in the second half of the decade, which was over $29 billion. Average inflows in the latter half of the decade were, therefore, nearly six times higher than those in the first half.

Figure 5.1: Average FDI Equity Inflows Reported during Different Periods, 1991–2010

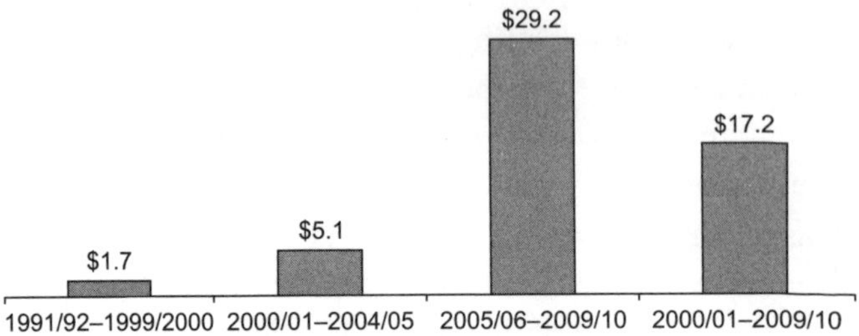

Source: *Database of the Indian Economy*, 2018, RBI, available at https://dbie.rbi.org.in/DBIE/dbie.rbi?site=statistics (accessed 5 August 2018). Based on 'Fact Sheet on Foreign Direct Investment (FDI)', DPIIT, December 2009 and November 2010.

Route-wise distribution of FDI inflows provides a perspective on the nature of FDI inflows through which foreign investors expanded their presence in the country (Table 5.6). The three major routes through which foreign investors brought in equity investment—namely the approvals route, through FIPB, automatic route and acquisitions route—and the trends in each of three

Table 5.6: Entry Route-wise Distribution of FDI Equity Inflows,# 2000–10 ($ Billion)

Year	*Direct Invest-ment to India*	*Equity**					*Reinvested Earnings*	*Other Capital*
		Total Equity	*Government (SIA/FIPB)*	*RBI*	*Acquisi-tion of Shares*	*Equity Capital of Unincor-porated Bodies*		
2000–01	4.0	2.4	1.5	0.5	0.4	0.1	1.4	0.3
2001–02	6.1	4.1	2.2	0.8	0.9	0.2	1.6	0.4
2002–03	5.0	2.8	0.9	0.7	0.9	0.2	1.8	0.4
2003–04	4.3	2.2	0.9	0.5	0.7	0.0	1.5	0.6
2004–05	6.1	3.8	1.1	1.3	0.9	0.5	1.9	0.4
2005–06	9.7	6.7	1.9	2.2	2.2	0.4	2.8	0.2
2006–07	22.8	16.5	2.2	7.2	6.3	0.9	5.8	0.5
2007–08	34.8	26.9	2.3	17.1	5.1	2.3	7.7	0.3
2008–09	41.9	32.1	5.4	21.3	4.6	0.7	9.0	0.8
2009–10	37.7	27.1	3.5	19.0	3.1	1.5	8.7	1.9

Notes: # Excluding investments in unincorporated bodies, reinvested earnings and other capital.

* Includes small quantities on account of NRI investment for the years 2000–01 and 2001–02.

Source: Based on *RBI Monthly Bulletin*, January 2011, Table 44.

routes are given in Table 5.6. The table shows that foreign investors' acquisition of domestic enterprises made important contributions to FDI equity inflows[9] from the beginning of the decade. This component peaked in 2005–06 and 2006–07, reaching almost two-fifths of the total FDI equity flows, but fell thereafter.

Acquisition of shares, which do not represent actual inflows and hence cannot create fresh capacities, together with reinvested earnings, accounted for a substantial proportion of the reported total inflows (Figure 5.2). Another notable feature of the inflows is that the proportion of the inflows subject to specific government approvals declined from 62.3 per cent in 2000–01 to 13.6 per cent in 2009–10, reflecting the progressively greater freedom enjoyed

Figure 5.2: Relative Contribution of Reinvested Earnings and Acquisition of Shares to FDI, 2001–10

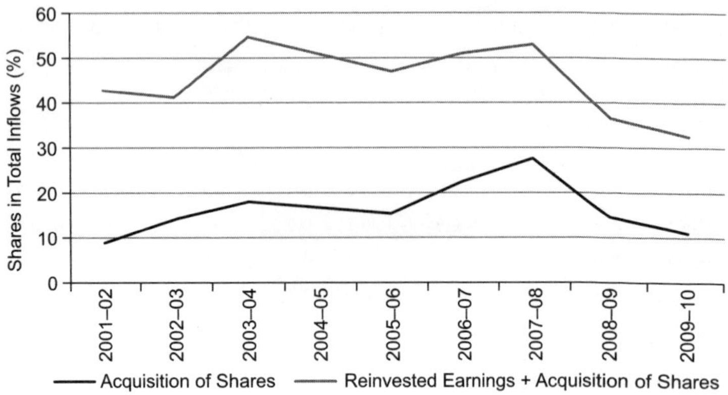

Source: Based on *RBI Monthly Bulletin*, January 2011, Table 44.

by foreign investors to invest in India without being subjected to government scrutiny. The corresponding increase in the share of investments which need mere reporting to the RBI at 74 per cent in 2009–10, substantiates the earlier point.

Sectoral Distribution

In assessing the sectoral distribution of FDI inflows in the 2000s, two sets of problems are encountered. The first is the inconsistency in the presentation of the official statistics. For example, in the earlier years of the decade, data on approved cases of FDI rather than actual inflows was available from DPIIT. Even when actual inflows were reported, the data was provided for calendar years as against financial years, which is usually the norm for reporting official statistics. The second problem is that the classification of approvals/inflows data was hampered by excessive aggregation and changes in the classification system over the years. Several years later, *Economic Survey 2014–15* commented on the anomaly thus: '[T]he ambiguity in classifying FDI in different activities under the services sector continues' (Government of India 2015: paragraph 7.15). Such ambiguity was amply visible in the official reporting for the period 2000–09, some samples of which are provided in Box 5.1.

Box 5.1 informs us about the problem areas arising from the classification of sectors in the official statistics. There are at least three problems that we would like to point out: the first is the overlap of sectors across the broad groupings. For instance, 'construction' is included both in groups I and II. Second, the residual category in several groups, namely 'others', was often reported to have the largest share in group, in case of the 'miscellaneous manufacturing industries'. 'Others' accounted for more than 50 per cent of the approvals/inflows during several years. And finally, the telecommunications sector includes an entry which suggests that some elements of broadcasting were also taken into consideration.

Box 5.1: Classification of Broad Sectors and their Components in Official Data on FDI

I. Miscellaneous manufacturing industries include:
(i) horticulture; (ii) agriculture (hybrid seeds and plantation); (iii) floriculture; (iv) diamond; (v) ornament and gold; (vi) construction activities and real estate; (vii) tea/coffee; (viii) cigarettes; (ix) printing of books, etc.; (x) coir; and (xi) others (miscellaneous industries).

II. Telecommunications include:
(i) telecommunications, (ii) radio paging; (iii) cellular mobile/basic telephone service; (iv) telecommunication (information and broadcasting); and (v) others (telecommunications).

III. Consultancy services include:
(i) design and engineering services, (ii) management services; (iii) marketing; (iv) construction; and (v) others (consultancy service).

Source: Compiled by the authors from the *SIA Newsletter* (renamed *FDI Newsletter*), various issues, DPIIT, available at https://dipp.gov.in/publications/si-news-letters/archives (accessed 5 August 2018).

Table 5.7 provides the data on sector-wise FDI approvals for the years 2000–01 to 2003–04 for the top-10 sectors.

Table 5.7: FDI Approvals in the Early Years of the 2000s ($ Million)

Industries	*2000–01*	*2001–02*	*2002–03*	*2003–04*
Engineering goods	2,236.2	680.8	267.9	291.7
Telecommunications	2,602.7	444.4	166.1	149.5
Trading	56.5	35.0	44.3	128.4
Services sectors	125.3	301.6	182.1	110.8
Chemicals	345.5	103.3	100.4	82.3
Fuels	1,130.2	1,110.7	65.9	48.8
Hotel and tourism	69.4	23.2	18.6	36.3
Processed food	40.9	106.4	149.3	22.9
Consultancy services	51.0	41.6	21.5	18.3
Metallurgical industries	316.5	156.5	13.1	7.1
Others	253.6	369.8	207.2	144.1
Total	7,227.8	3,373.3	1,236.4	1,040.3

Source: Compiled by the authors from the *SIA Newsletter* (renamed *FDI Newsletter*), various issues, DPIIT, available at https://dipp.gov.in/publications/si-news-letters/archives (accessed 5 August 2018).

Table 5.7 indicates that the approvals for foreign investment were highly concentrated in the top-10 sectors, accounting for 83–96 per cent of the total approvals. Telecommunications, engineerng goods and fuels dominated the approvals in all the four years.

Table 5.8 provides the distribution of FDI approvals across sectors. An interesting shift away from manufacturing and towards services can be seen from the figures. This indicates that foreign investors reinforced the movement towards the modern services sector that was seen in India from the early years of the millennium.

We would like to emphasise at this point that the figures provided here are mere indications of the trends in the likely involvement of foreign investors in India. We have already clarified that these figures represent approvals granted by the government

Table 5.8: Distribution of Approved Foreign Investment between Broad Sectors, 2000–04 (%)

Industries	*2000–01*	*2001–02*	*2002–03*	*2003–04*
Agriculture	0.3	0.4	0.2	0.5
Manufacturing	58.1	70.7	54.3	45.3
Services	40.2	25.1	35.0	42.6
Unclassified	1.4	3.8	10.4	11.5

Source: Compiled by the authors from the *SIA Newsletter* (renamed *FDI Newsletter*), various issues, DPIIT, available at https://dipp.gov.in/publications/si-news-letters/archives (accessed 5 August 2018).

that have been used in the absence of data on sector-wise actual inflows for the years mentioned in Table 5.8. A second point we would make is that the approvals data became a weak proxy for the participation of foreign companies because of the slackening of government regulations over foreign investors.

Sectoral Distribution of FDI Inflows

We will now consider the sectoral distribution of actual flows of FDI. DPIIT provides data for the major sectors receiving equity inflows from the year 2004–05. Table 5.9 provides the data for the top-10 sectors until the end of the 2000s.

Table 5.9: FDI Inflows in the Top-10 Sectors, 2004–10 ($ Million)

Sectors	*2004–05*	*2005–06*	*2006–07*	*2007–08*	*2008–09*	*2009–10*
Services sector (financial and non-financial)	444	543	4,664	6,615	6,116	4,392
Computer software and hardware	539	1,375	2,614	1,410	1,677	919
Housing and real estate	0	38	467	2,179	2,801	2,844
Construction activities (including roads and highways)	152	151	985	1,743	2,028	2,868

(Contd)

Table 5.9 (Contd)

Sectors	*2004–05*	*2005–06*	*2006–07*	*2007–08*	*2008–09*	*2009–10*
Telecommunications (radio paging, cellular mobile, basic telephone services)	125	624	478	1,261	2,558	2,554
Power	53	87	157	967	985	1,437
Automobile industry	122	143	276	675	1,152	1,177
Metallurgical industries	182	147	173	1,177	961	407
Petroleum and natural gas	113	14	89	1,427	412	272
Chemicals (other than fertilisers)	198	390	205	229	749	362
Total for the top-10 sectors (% share in equity inflows)	1,928 (59.3)	3,512 (63.4)	10,108 (64.9)	17,683 (72.0)	19,439 (71.1)	17,232 (67.3)

Source: Compiled by the authors from the *SIA Newsletter* (renamed *FDI Newsletter*), various issues, DPIIT, available at https://dipp.gov.in/publications/si-news-letters/archives (accessed 5 August 2018).

Increased FDI inflows after the mid-2000s were accompanied by a significant development: the confirmation that the services sectors were major recipients of FDI. During 2004–05 to 2009–10, four of the top-five sectors that attracted the largest equity inflows for the period taken as a whole belonged to the services sector.[10] Within services, financial services had the largest share in the group of the top-10 (almost a third), while construction and real estate gained the most after 2007–08 (Table 5.9 and Figure 5.3). A further scrutiny of the data suggests that only a few of the Indian investee companies like Punj Lloyd, Soma Enterprises and Shriram EPC can be categorised as engineering and construction companies, and the rest are developers—a few of these were engaged in setting up IT parks and SEZs. A similar examination of the inflows in the financial sector suggested that close to 40 per cent of the inflows were into companies that served the securities market, suggesting that they did not directly contribute to the long-term financing

Figure 5.3: Distribution of Foreign Equity Inflows, 2007–10#

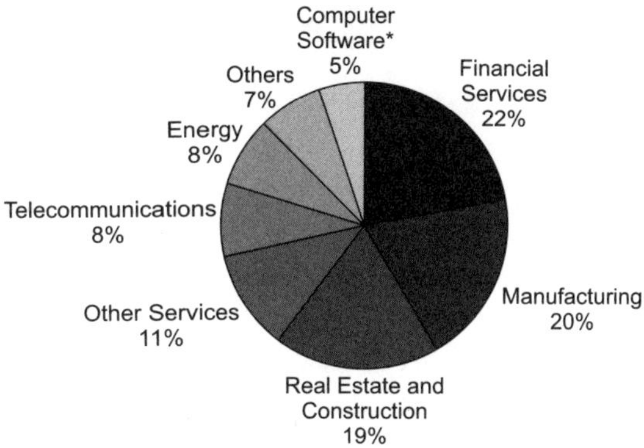

Notes: # Excluding those into unincorporated bodies, reinvested earnings and other capital.

* Following the previous year's distribution, the share of computer software within the broad classification of 'Computer software and hardware' has been taken approximately as 96%.

Source: Compiled by the authors from the *SIA Newsletter* (renamed *FDI Newsletter*), various issues, DPIIT, available at https://dipp.gov.in/publications/si-news-letters/archives (accessed 5 August 2018).

needs of Indian business. These could be termed as adjuncts to the foreign portfolio investors.

Table 5.10 provides a more detailed account of FDI inflows by sectors and industries, taking advantage of the significantly better reporting by the DPIIT in the second half of the 2000s. Two trends can be seen from the table: the dominance of the services sector and the diminished role of the manufacturing sector. Within the services sector, financial services and real estate and construction received nearly three-fourths of the total inflows in the services sector, and more than 40 per cent of the overall inflows during 2007–10. The priorities of the foreign investors are quite evident from these numbers.

The most noticeable aspect of the trends in inflows was the steady shift away from manufacturing from the middle of the 2000s, a trend that was strengthened by the end of the decade.

Table 5.10: FDI Inflows in Major Sectors/Industries, 2007–10 ($ Billion)

Sectors/Industries	*2007–08*	*2008–09*	*2009–10*	2007–10
Services sector	15.4	17.9	17.4	50.7
Financial services	6.6	6.1	4.4	17.1
Real estate and construction	2.2	2.8	2.8	7.8
Telecommunications	1.7	2.0	2.9	6.6
Computer software	1.3	2.6	2.6	6.4
Trading	1.4	1.7	0.9	4.0
Hotel and tourism	0.6	0.6	0.6	1.8
Information and broadcasting (including print media)	0.4	0.4	0.7	1.6
Manufacturing	4.6	5.8	4.8	15.2
Automobile industry	0.7	1.2	1.2	3.0
Metallurgical industries	1.2	1.0	0.4	2.5
Electrical equipment	0.6	0.4	0.7	1.7
Chemicals (other than fertilisers)	0.2	0.7	0.4	1.3
Cement and gypsum products	0.02	0.7	0.03	0.8
Drugs and pharmaceuticals	0.3	0.2	0.2	0.7
Industrial machinery	0.1	0.1	0.4	0.6
Energy	2.5	1.5	2.2	6.1
Power	1.0	1.0	1.4	3.4
Petroleum and natural gas	1.4	0.4	0.3	2.1
Non-conventional energy	0.04	0.1	0.5	0.6
Others	2.1	2.2	1.4	5.7
Miscellaneous industries	0.6	1.5	1.0	3.2
Ports	0.9	0.5	0.1	1.5
Mining	0.4	0.03	0.2	0.7
Total	24.6	27.3	25.8	77.7

Source: Compiled by the authors from the *SIA Newsletter* (renamed *FDI Newsletter*), various issues, DPIIT, available at https://dipp.gov.in/publications/si-news-letters/archives (accessed 5 August 2018).

This trend is particularly significant since around this phase, Government of India had started taking note of the low share of manufacturing in the country's GDP: it was about 17–18 per cent of the GDP. In 2006, the National Manufacturing Competitiveness Council (Government of India 2006: 59) commented in its report that the share of manufacturing in GDP should increase to at least 23 per cent by 2015 from the then-existing level. Although successive governments progressively removed entry barriers for foreign investors in the manufacturing sector, expecting that these investors would help revive its sagging fortunes, foreign investors did not respond to the priorities of the government (Table 5.11). The share of FDI inflows in the manufacturing sector registered a steep fall from 61 per cent in 2004–05 to less than a fifth in 2009–10.

Table 5.11: Changing Sectoral Shares in FDI Equity Inflows, 2004–10 (%)

Sectors	*2004–05*	*2005–06*	*2006–07*	*2007–08*	*2008–09*	*2009–10*
Manufacturing	61.0	52.3	25.1	18.7	21.2	18.6
Services	29.8	36.2	62.1	62.8	65.4	67.5
Energy	0.0	1.7	1.5	10.0	5.4	8.5
Miscellaneous industries	9.2	9.7	11.3	8.5	8.0	5.4
Total	100.0	100.0	100.0	100.0	100.0	100.0

Source: Compiled by the authors from the *SIA Newsletter* (renamed *FDI Newsletter*), various issues, DPIIT, available at https://dipp.gov.in/publications/si-news-letters/archives (accessed 5 August 2018).

Sources of FDI Inflows in the 2000s

As for the source countries of FDI in India, the 2000s showed a clear shift towards established tax havens like Mauritius and Singapore (Table 5.12). We mentioned earlier that Mauritius had emerged as one of the top sources of equity inflows towards the end of the 1990s, and its position was further strengthened in the following decade. During the period 2002–03 to 2009–10, Mauritius accounted for more than 40 per cent of the total reported inflows. What also needs to be highlighted here is that most of India's source countries figured prominently in the

Table 5.12: India's FDI Equity Inflows: Top-10 Home Countries Share, 2002–10 (%)

Countries	*2002–03 to 2004–05*	*2005–06 to 2007–08*	*2008–09 to 2009–10*	*2002–03 to 2009–10*
Mauritius*	26.1	44.7	40.6	41.0
Singapore*	2.7	8.8	11.0	9.3
US	14.2	5.5	7.0	7.0
UK	6.4	7.4	2.9	5.1
Netherlands	9.8	3.2	3.3	3.8
Cyprus	0.0	2.0	5.5	3.5
Japan	6.5	2.5	3.0	3.1
Germany	3.9	2.1	2.4	2.4
UAE*	0.0	1.2	1.7	1.3
France	0.0	0.6	1.4	1.0
Total for top-10	58.6	72.6	71.6	70.9

Note: * Excluding NRI investments and those for which country details have not been reported. The ranking is based on their position from 2002–03 to 2009–10.

Source: Based on the data provided in the *SIA Newsletter*, various monthly and annual issues. Classification of home countries into tax havens is based on Tax Justice Network (2007) and United States Government Accountability Office (2008).

2011 Financial Secrecy Index of the Tax Justice Network, which identified jurisdictions having less than desirable transparency in their financial market regulations, and could therefore be called 'tax havens' (Tax Justice Network 2011).

It is not just the top-10 countries that bring questionable sources of FDI into India; the problem is, in fact, considerably bigger. This issue is especially relevant because policymakers in India have been emphasising on the developmental role of FDI. However, if the list of more than 90 countries from which India received FDI between 2002–03 and 2009–10 were perused, one would find that a significant number of these countries were not those that could have provided the bundle of intangibles like technology and other inputs that are necessary for strengthening India's manufacturing sectors (Table 5.13). A second area of concern is that many of these countries are either failed states or tax havens. A more detailed analysis of this aspect of the sources of FDI will be provided in the following section.

Table 5.13: Sources of FDI in India with Doubtful Records as Providers of Finance

Bahamas	Libya
Bermuda	Maldives
British Isles	Mauritius
British Virginia	Myanmar
Cayman Island	Nevis
Colombia	Nicosia
Cyprus	Nigeria
Djibouti	Panama
East Africa	Seychelles
Fiji Islands	St. Vincent
Gibraltar	Sudan
Iran	UAE
Jordon	Vanuatu
Kazakhstan	Virgin Islands
Kenya	West Africa
North Korea	West Indies
Kyrgyzstan	Yemen
Lebanon	Zambia
Liberia	

Source: Compiled by the authors from the *SIA Newsletter* (renamed *FDI Newsletter*), various issues, DPIIT, available at https://dipp.gov.in/publications/si-news-letters/archives (accessed 5 August 2018).

FDI Trends in the 2010s

FDI inflows into India expanded significantly after 2012–13. In the early years of the decade, FDI inflows were subdued as the persisting effects of the economic recession of 2008 were being felt by the global economy (Table 5.14 and Figure 5.4).

Table 5.14: Entry Route-wise Distribution of FDI Equity Inflows, 2010–18 ($ Billion)

Year	*Gross Inflows*	*Equity Capital*					*Reinvested Earnings*	*Other Capital*
		Total Equity	*Government (SIA/FIPB)*	*RBI*	*Acquisition of Shares*	*Equity Capital of Unincorporated Bodies*		
2010–11	34.8	22.3	1.9	13.0	6.4	0.9	11.9	0.7
2011–12	46.6	35.9	3.0	20.4	11.4	1.0	8.2	2.5
2012–13	34.3	22.9	2.3	16.0	3.5	1.1	9.9	1.5
2013–14	36.0	25.3	1.2	14.9	8.2	1.0	9.0	1.8
2014–15	45.1	31.9	2.2	22.5	6.2	1.0	10.0	3.2
2015–16	55.6	41.1	3.6	32.5	3.9	1.1	10.4	4.0
2016–17	60.2	44.7	5.9	30.4	7.2	1.2	12.3	3.2
2017–18	61.0	45.5	7.8	29.6	7.5	0.7	12.5	2.9

Source: *RBI Bulletin*, various issues.

Figure 5.4: Trends in FDI Inflows, 2010–18

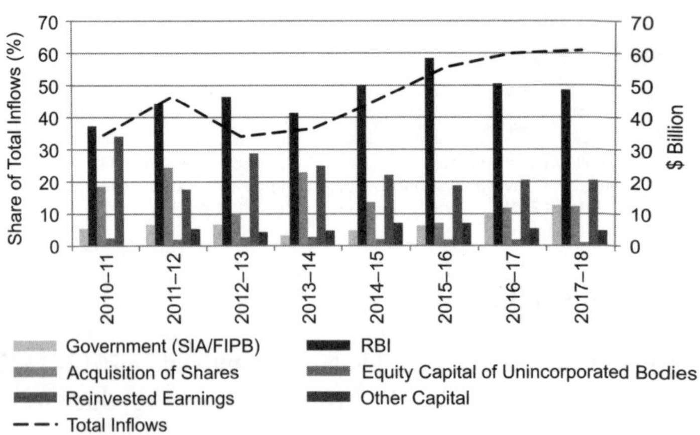

Source: *RBI Bulletin*, various issues.

FDI inflows rose sharply by 25 per cent in 2014–15, but in the subsequent years, there was a marked slowing of the growth of inflows. The numbers for 2017–18 were mired in confusion, with the DPIIT and RBI giving different sets of numbers.[11]

Equity inflows increased significantly since the beginning of 2010s, doubling between 2010–11 and 2016–17. Inflows through the 'automatic route' (RBI) also doubled during the same period, indicating, as in the earlier decades, the extent of relaxation of FDI policies and greater freedom enjoyed by foreign investors in making their investment decisions. Acquisition of shares and reinvested earnings taken together accounted for just less than a third in 2017–18, after reaching a peak of over 42 per cent in 2011–12

Sectoral Distribution of FDI Equity Inflows

Inflows of equity capital continued to be highly concentrated in the services sector during the 2010s, confirming a trend that was established in the previous decade (Table 5.15). Financial services were the overwhelming favourites of foreign investors; the sweeping relaxation of government controls over most areas in the financial sector paved way for the strong penetration of foreign capital. The relatively low level of exposure of India's financial sector to the global capital markets was one of the main reasons why the earlier episodes of financial crises did not adversely affect the country's economy. This situation changed completely a decade since the last major global economic downturn in 2008. The pattern of inflows can be seen in Table 5.15.

Alongside the consolidation of the services sector as the favoured sector for foreign investors, the share of the manufacturing sector in the total FDI inflows declined continuously after 2013–14. In 2017–18, the share of the manufacturing sector declined

Table 5.15: Distribution of FDI Equity Inflows across Sectors, 2010–18 ($ Million)

Sectors	*2010–11*	*2011–12*	*2012–13*	*2013–14*	*2014–15*	*2015–16*	*2016–17*	*2017–18*	*2010–11 to 2017–18*
Services	10.4	14.9	12.5	10.0	15.6	27.6	27.2	32.2	150.4
*Financial services**	3.4	5.2	4.8	2.2	3.3	6.9	8.7	6.7	41.2
Telecommunications	1.7	2.0	0.3	1.3	2.9	1.3	5.6	6.2	21.3
Computer software and hardware	0.8	0.8	0.5	1.1	2.2	5.9	3.7	6.2	21.1
Trading	0.5	0.8	0.7	1.3	2.8	3.8	2.3	4.3	16.6
Construction activities	1.1	0.4	0.3	0.5	0.9	4.5	1.9	2.7	12.2
Hotel and tourism	0.3	1.0	3.3	0.5	0.8	1.3	0.9	1.1	9.2
Construction development	0.0	3.1	1.3	1.2	0.8	0.1	0.1	0.5	7.2
Information and broadcasting	0.4	0.7	0.4	0.4	0.3	1.0	1.5	0.6	5.3
Hospital and diagnostic centres	0.3	0.3	0.3	0.7	0.7	0.7	0.7	0.7	4.4
Manufacturing	5.5	15.1	7.8	12.2	11.3	9.5	13.9	9.3	84.5
Automobile industry	1.3	0.9	1.5	1.5	2.6	2.5	1.6	2.1	14.1
Chemicals (other than fertilisers)	0.4	4.0	0.3	0.8	0.7	1.5	1.4	1.3	10.4
Drugs and pharmaceuticals	0.2	3.2	1.1	1.3	1.5	0.8	0.9	1.0	10.0
Metallurgical industries	1.1	1.8	1.5	0.6	0.5	0.5	1.4	0.4	7.7
Food processing industries	0.2	0.2	0.4	4.0	0.5	0.5	0.7	0.9	7.4

(Contd)

Table 5.15 (Contd)

Sectors	*2010–11*	*2011–12*	*2012–13*	*2013–14*	*2014–15*	*2015–16*	*2016–17*	*2017–18*	*2010–11 to 2017–18*
Electrical equipment	0.2	0.6	0.2	0.1	0.6	0.4	2.2	0.5	4.8
Industrial machinery	0.6	0.6	0.5	0.5	0.9	0.6	0.3	0.5	4.4
Energy	2.0	4.1	1.9	1.6	2.3	1.7	2.1	2.8	18.6
Power	1.3	1.7	0.5	1.1	0.7	0.9	1.1	1.6	8.8
Non-conventional energy	0.2	0.5	1.1	0.4	0.6	0.8	0.8	1.2	5.5
Petroleum and natural gas	0.6	2.0	0.2	0.1	1.1	0.1	0.2	0.0	4.3
Others	1.5	1.0	0.3	0.5	1.6	1.2	0.4	0.4	7.0
Total	19.4	35.1	22.4	24.3	30.9	40.0	43.5	44.9	260.5

Note: * Also includes outsourcing, research and development (R&D), courier, technical testing and analysis, etc.

Source: Compiled by the authors from the *SIA Newsletter* (renamed *FDI Newsletter*), various issues, DPIIT, available at https://dipp.gov.in/publications/si-news-letters/archives (accessed 5 August 2018).

Table 5.16: Share of the Broad Sectors in FDI Inflows, 2010–18

Sectors	*2010–11*	*2011–12*	*2012–13*	*2013–14*	*2014–15*	*2015–16*	*2016–17*	*2017–18*	*2010–11 to 2017–18*
Services	53.6	42.4	55.6	41.3	50.6	68.9	62.5	71.8	57.7
Manufacturing	28.1	43.0	34.7	50.1	36.6	23.6	31.9	20.8	32.5
Energy	10.4	11.8	8.3	6.6	7.6	4.4	4.8	6.4	7.1
Others	7.9	2.8	1.4	2.0	5.2	3.1	0.8	1.0	2.7

Source: Compiled by the authors from the *SIA Newsletter* (renamed *FDI Newsletter*), various issues, DPIIT, available at https://dipp.gov.in/publications/si-news-letters/archives (accessed 5 August 2018).

to 20.8 per cent, its lowest for the decade (Table 5.16). Since the middle of the previous decade, successive governments have spoken about the importance of increasing the share of the manufacturing sector, from mid- to high-teens to at least a fourth of the GDP.[12] Figures in the Table 5.16 show that foreign investors were reluctant participants in the government's initiatives for the revival of the manufacturing sector.

'Make in India' and FDI Inflows

The National Democratic Alliance (NDA) government unveiled 'Make in India' as its first major programme for transforming the Indian economy. The primary goal of this initiative was to transform India into a global manufacturing hub, which was to be achieved by increasing the share of manufacturing in the country's GDP to 25 per cent in 2025 (Government of India 2016a), or by about 10 percentage points. In order to lend a better focus to this initiative, the government identified 25 sectors, of which 13 were in the manufacturing sector, while the rest belonged to the services and infrastructure sectors (Table 5.17).

Table 5.17: 'Make in India' Sectors

Automobile	Food processing	Renewable energy
Automobile components	IT and business process management	Roads and highways
Aviation	Leather	Space
Biotechnology	Media and entertainment	Textiles and garments
Chemicals	Mining	Thermal power
Construction	Oil and gas	Tourism and hospitality
Defence manufacturing	Pharmaceuticals	Wellness
Electrical machinery	Ports and shipping	
Electronic systems	Railways	

Source: Compiled from the Make in India website, available at http://www.makeinindia.com/sectors (accessed 31 May 2018).

Although the statement of intent of 'Make in India' spoke of encouraging both 'multinational as well as domestic companies to manufacture their products within the country' (Government of India 2016a), liberalisation of FDI policies that the NDA government began in August 2014 suggested a new level of confidence that it developed in the ability of the foreign companies to contribute to the 'making of India'. This was more than evident from the following unequivocal statement of the government: 'FDI reforms reflect a decisive change in philosophy, from viewing FDI as a tolerable necessity to something to welcome'. Operationally, FDI policy reforms were intended to 'put more and more FDI proposals on automatic route instead of Government route where time and energy of the investors is wasted' (Government of India 2016b: 2).

The response of foreign investors to the 'Make in India' initiative is captured in Table 5.18. Except for the space sector, equity inflows into all the other sectors included in the initiative are shown in the table.

Table 5.18: Foreign Equity Inflows into the 'Make in India' Sectors, 2014–18 ($ Billion)

Make in India Sectors	*2014–15*	*2015–16*	*2016–17*	*2017–18*	*2014–15 to 2017–18*
Thermal power	0.7	0.9	1.1	1.4	4.3
Renewable energy	0.6	0.8	0.8	1.2	3.4
Oil and gas	1.1	0.1	0.2	0.0	1.4
Automobile	2.6	2.5	1.6	2.1	8.8
Chemicals	0.7	1.5	1.4	1.3	4.8
Biotechnology/pharmaceuticals	1.5	0.8	0.9	1.0	4.1
Electrical machinery	0.6	0.4	2.2	0.5	3.7
Food processing	0.5	0.5	0.7	0.9	2.7
Textiles and garments	0.2	0.2	0.6	0.4	1.5
Electronic systems	0.1	0.2	0.1	0.2	0.6
Railways	0.1	0.1	0.1	0.1	0.4
Leather	0.04	0.02	0.00	0.02	0.08
Defence manufacturing	0.0	0.0	0.0	0.0	neg.*
Mining	0.7	0.5	0.1	0.0	1.3
IT and business process management	2.2	5.9	3.7	6.2	17.9
Tourism and hospitality	0.8	1.3	0.9	1.1	4.2
Media and entertainment	0.3	1.0	1.5	0.6	3.4
Wellness	0.7	0.7	0.7	0.7	2.9
Ports and shipping	0.3	0.4	0.7	1.0	2.5
Construction/roads and highways	1.6	4.6	2.0	3.3	11.1
Aviation	0.1	0.4	0.1	0.6	1.1
Total for Make in India sectors	15.2	22.9	19.4	22.6	80.0
Total equity inflows	30.9	40.0	43.5	44.9	159.3

Note: * Less than $200,000

Source: Compiled by the authors from the *SIA Newsletter* (renamed *FDI Newsletter*), various issues, DPIIT, available at https://dipp.gov.in/publications/si-news-letters/archives (accessed 5 August 2018).

Given their preference for the services sector in general, foreign investors backed the services sectors figuring in the 'Make in India' initiative as well. Nearly 54 per cent of the FDI inflows between 2014–15 and 2017–18 went into the services sectors. However, more than 40 per cent of the inflows into this sector were accounted for by the IT and business process management sectors, and a further 25 per cent went into construction and roads/highways. In other words, two of the sectors saw disproportionately large interest from foreign investors.

As with the earlier initiatives for reviving the fortunes of the manufacturing sector through greater infusion of foreign investment, the 'Make in India' initiative, too, received a hesitant response. During the period of implementation of the initiative, the manufacturing sector received a third of the total FDI inflows. Perhaps more disconcertingly, the share of this sector in the total inflows declined in 2017–18.

Sources of Inflows

Equity inflows into India came largely from a similar set of countries, as in the previous decade. Table 5.19 provides the details.

Table 5.19: Top Sources of FDI Inflows, 2010–18

Countries	*FDI Inflows ($ Billion)*	*Share in Total FDI Inflows (%)*
Mauritius	80.3	30.1
Singapore	56.6	21.2
Japan	23.6	8.8
Netherlands	19.0	7.1
UK	19.6	7.3
US	14.1	5.3
Germany	8.0	3.0
Cyprus	5.7	2.1
France	4.7	1.8
UAE	4.2	1.6

(Contd)

Table 5.19 (Contd)

Countries	*FDI Inflows ($ Billion)*	*Share in Total FDI Inflows (%)*
Switzerland	3.4	1.3
Hong Kong SAR	2.6	1.0
Luxembourg	2.4	0.9
Spain	2.1	0.8
South Korea	2.1	0.8
Cayman Islands	2.1	0.8
Italy	1.8	0.7
China	1.9	0.7
Belgium	1.0	0.4
Total for these countries	255.1	95.7
Total equity inflows	266.6	100.0

Source: Compiled by the authors from the *SIA Newsletter* (renamed *FDI Newsletter*), various issues, DPIIT, available at https://dipp.gov.in/publications/si-news-letters/archives (accessed 5 August 2018).

Table 5.19 includes 19 countries that contributed a billion dollars or more in the total FDI inflows. The share of these countries was more than 95 per cent of the total FDI inflows. In fact, the top-five countries, namely Mauritius, Singapore, Japan, the Netherlands and the UK, accounted for three-fourths of the total inflows.

Mauritius remained the top source of FDI inflows, but in recent years, its gap with the second largest source, namely Singapore, has decreased considerably. This happened after the government took serious note of the contention that inflows of capital from Mauritius were violating the Double Taxation Avoidance Agreement between the two countries, as well as the General Anti-avoidance Rules (GAAR) introduced in 2012 to prevent tax avoidance. When the issue of GAAR was in sharp focus following its introduction, inflows from Mauritius declined to $5 billion in 2013–14, putting this source country behind Singapore. But in the year 2017–18, when GAAR was finally implemented, FDI inflows from Mauritius increased to nearly $16.0 billion, almost twice the level of the immediately preceding fiscal year, and its share went up from 29 per cent in 2014–15 to more than 35 per cent in 2017–18.

As compared to the earlier phases of the post-1991 period, the sources from which India received equity investment during the current decade have seen both quantitative and qualitative changes. First, the quantitative aspect: 148 countries have invested in India in the decade of the 2010s, well above 91 countries that did so in the preceding decade. The number of countries providing FDI has increased significantly, in step with the investment liberalisation, suggesting yet again a clear relationship between easing of controls on foreign investors and an expansion in the sources of funding.

Now to the qualitative aspect of the change in the sources of funding: we mentioned earlier that several countries providing such funds were not exactly those from which Indian industry could expect to receive advanced technology and other assets for increasing its competitiveness. In addition to countries with a doubtful record as suppliers of capital, as listed in Table 5.13, suppliers of FDI to India in recent years have included Afghanistan, Algeria, the Democratic Republic of Congo, Senegal, Iraq, the Isle of Man, the Togolese Republic and Syria.

Trends in Repatriation of Capital

One phenomenon which emerged in the 2000s, and which has gained considerable significance in recent years, is the repatriation of capital by foreign investors. Until the end of the 2000s, repatriation of capital was less than $5 billion dollars, having been less than a billion dollars in the earlier years.

Table 5.20: Trends in Repatriation of Capital, 2004–18 ($ Billion, Unless Qualified)

Years	*FDI Inflows*	*Equity Inflows*	*Repatriation/Disinvestment*	
			Total	*Equity*
2004–05	6.1	3.8	0.1 (1.1)*	0.1 (1.7)**
2005–06	9.7	6.7	0.1 (0.6)*	0.1 (0.9)**
2006–07	22.8	16.5	0.1 (0.4)*	0.1 (0.5)**
2007–08	34.8	26.9	0.1 (0.3)*	0.1 (0.4)**
2008–09	41.9	32.1	0.2 (0.4)*	0.2 (0.5)**
2009–10	37.7	27.1	4.6 (12.3)*	4.2 (15.6)**
2010–11	34.8	22.3	7.0 (20.1)*	6.5 (29.3)**
2011–12	46.6	35.9	13.6 (29.2)*	13.0 (36.3)**
2012–13	34.3	22.9	7.3 (21.4)*	6.9 (29.9)**
2013–14	36.0	25.3	5.3 (14.7)*	4.8 (18.9)**
2014–15	45.1	31.9	9.9 (21.8)*	9.6 (30.1)**
2015–16	55.6	41.1	10.7 (19.2)*	10.5 (25.6)**
2016–17	60.2	44.7	18.0 (29.9)*	17.3 (38.7)**
2017–18	56.8	42.2	19.1 (33.6)*	18.9 (44.7)**

Notes: * Figures in parentheses are percentage of FDI inflows.

** Figures in parentheses are percentage of equity inflows.

Source: *Database on Indian Economy*, RBI, available at https://dbie.rbi.org.in/DBIE/dbie.rbi?site=statistics (accessed 5 August 2018).

Table 5.20 shows the alarming pace at which repatriation of capital has taken place, especially since 2013–14. As a share of FDI inflows, total repatriation in 2013–14 was just less than 22 per cent, but by 2017–18, this figure had increased to nearly 34 per cent. Repatriation of equity capital was even more serious. This largest component of FDI inflows saw repatriation of nearly 30 per cent of equity inflows in 2014–15, which increased to close to 45 per cent in 2017–18. This implies that foreign investors had withdrawn equity capital measuring almost half of inflows for the year. Consequently, net inflows of FDI registered a relatively small increase since 2014–15.

Notes

1. As mentioned in Chapter 4, Government of India established the FIPB following the Statement of Industrial Policy in 1991 which was an inter-ministerial agency responsible for vetting FDI proposals. FIPB was phased out in 2018–19.

2. The acquisition of shares of Indian companies by non-residents through private arrangements was included as part of FDI since January 1996 (RBI 2010: 83).

3. FDI approvals were nearly $200 million in 1989. Our estimates show that the actual inflows during the early 1990s were approximately 25 per cent of the amount for which the government had granted approvals. This gives us the estimated amount of inflows for this year.

4. Much of the initial inflows were on account of the hike in equity to majority by the existing foreign companies. At the end of January 1995, equity-hike cases accounted for 53.8 per cent of the inflows. The realisation in their case was 73.3 per cent. In all other cases, it was only 19 per cent.

5. We mentioned earlier that for the 1990s and the early years of the 2000s, DIPP did not provide the actual inflows data while reporting the sectoral composition of FDI—the available data pertained to the approvals granted by the government. The data is, therefore, proposed investments and not actual investments.

6. The framework was provided by the Industrial Policy Resolution of 1956. Most of the key sectors were reserved for the public sector, which was expected to control the 'commanding heights of the economy' (Government of India 1991: paragraph 15).

7. There is, however, another dimension to it. In the early years, several expatriate Indians (for example, Swraj Paul and the Hindujas) promised huge investments, but these did not get translated into actual investments because their demands for favourable terms were not acceded to by the authorities/public sector partners, Indian Oil Corporation and Kuwait Petroleum (Institute for Studies in Industrial Development 1995).

8. India adopted the international practice of reporting FDI inflows data following the recommendations of the Committee on Compilation of Foreign Direct Investment in India, October 2002 (Government of India 2002).

9. Inflows through the FIPB/SIA, automatic and acquisition routes.

10. The group 'computer software and hardware' mostly included computer software.

11. While the DPIIT has reported that FDI inflows in 2017–18 were nearly $62 billion, RBI has produced three sets of numbers, one of which says that inflows were $56.8 billion, lower than the previous year's figure by nearly 6 per cent. See Rao and Dhar (2018).

12. We mentioned earlier that the National Manufacturing Competitiveness Council had, in its report, argued that the share of the manufacturing sector in GDP should increase to 23 per cent, resulting from its annual growth of 12 per cent. In 2011, the government announced a National Manufacturing Policy with the objective of raising the share of manufacturing in GDP to 25 per cent. The following government announced the biggest and the most detailed policy for the revival of the manufacturing sector, namely the 'Make in India' initiative, within months of its coming into power in 2014. Make in India identified 25 sectors, aimed at transforming 'India into a global design and manufacturing hub' (Government of India 2016a).

References

Akhtar, Jahanzeb and Verónica Grondona. 2019. 'Tax Haven Listing in Multiple Hues: Blind, Winking or Conniving?'. Research paper no. 94, South Centre, Geneva. Available at https://www.southcentre.int/wp-content/uploads/2019/04/RP94_Tax-Haven-Listing-in-Multiple-Hues-Blind-Winking-or-Conniving_EN.pdf (accessed 1 May 2019).

DPIIT. 2019. 'Foreign Direct Investment Policy'. Available at http://dipp.nic.in/policies-rules-and-acts/policies/foreign-direct-investment-policy (accessed 1 May 2019).

Government of India. 1991. 'Statement on Industrial Policy'. Department for Promotion of Industry and Internal Trade, 24 July. Available at https://dipp.gov.in/sites/default/files/chap001_0_0.pdf (accessed 25 July 2018).

______. 1995. 'SIA Newsletter: Volume 3, No. 9'. January. Ministry of Industry, Department of Industrial Development.

______. 2002. 'Committee on Compilation of Foreign Direct Investment in India'. Department of Industrial Policy and Promotion, October. Available at http://dipp.nic.in/sites/default/files/fdi.pdf (accessed 25 July 2018).

______. 2006. 'The National Strategy for Manufacturing'. National Manufacturing Competitiveness Council, New Delhi.

______. 2015. *Economic Survey 2014–15*, Volume 2. Ministry of Finance, Department of Economic Affairs. Available at https://www.indiabudget.gov.in/budget2015-2016/es2014-15/echapter-vol2.pdf (accessed 20 July 2018).

______. 2016a. 'Make in India: The Vision, New Processes, Sectors, Infrastructure and Mindset'. *Make in India*. Available at http://www.makeinindia.com/article/-/v/make-in-india-reason-vision-for-the-initiative (accessed 30 July 2018).

______. 2016b. Economic Survey 2015–16, Volume 1. Ministry of Finance.

Institute for Studies in Industrial Development. 1995. 'Foreign Investment Approvals and Implementation Status: A Review (August 1991 to December 1994)'. Project report for the Department of Economic Affairs, Ministry of Finance, March. Available at http://isid.org.in/pdf/FIA9194u.pdf (accessed 30 June 2018).

Kust, Matthew J. 1964. *Foreign Enterprise in India: Laws and Policies*. Chapel Hill, North Carolina: University of North Carolina Press.

Rao, K. S Chalapati and Biswajit Dhar. 2018. 'India's Recent Inward Foreign Direct Investment: An Assessment'. Institute for Studies in Industrial Development, New Delhi.

RBI. 2007. 'Manual on Financial and Banking Statistics'. Mumbai. Available at https://m.rbi.org.in/Scripts/AnnualPublications.aspx?head=Manual%20on%20Financial%20and%20Banking%20Statistics%20-%20March%202007 (accessed 10 July 2018).

RBI. 2010. 'Report of the Working Group on Balance of Payments Manual for India'. September. Available at https://www.rbi.org.in/scripts/PublicationReportDetails.aspx?UrlPage=&ID=596 (accessed 10 July 2018).

Tax Justice Network. 2007. 'Closing the Floodgates: Collecting Tax to Pay for Development'. Commissioned by the Norwegian Ministry of Foreign Affairs.

_____. 2011. 'The Significance of the 2011 Financial Secrecy Index'. Available at https://www.financialsecrecyindex.com/Archive2011/FSI-2011/FSI-Significance.pdf (accessed 1 May 2019).

United States Government Accountability Office. 2008. 'Large U.S. Corporations and Federal Contractors with Subsidiaries in Jurisdictions Listed as Tax Havens or Financial Privacy Jurisdictions'. Report to Congressional Requesters, December.

six

Performance of FDI Companies

A Brief Assessment

This chapter attempts to assess the performance of FDI companies in India during 2012–13 to 2017–18. This is a period for which we have a consistent set of data for FDI companies. This exercise is constrained by data limitations arising from two sets of issues. The first is that many FDI companies have not listed their shares in the stock market, and these companies are not required to make data regarding their functioning publicly available.[1] The second issue is that the standards of reporting have been changing which has contributed to considerable data gaps.

Given these limitations, we relied on two data sources to assess the performance of FDI companies. The first set of data is from the RBI's Annual Census on Foreign Liabilities and Assets of Indian Companies, and the second is from the Prowess database[2] that includes data from the annual reports of companies.

The Coordinated Direct Investment Survey (CDIS) began in 2009 'to improve the quality of direct investment position statistics in the international investment position (IIP) and the availability of these statistics by immediate counterpart economies' (IMF 2015: 1). Thus, comparable data on FDI is now available for about 100 countries. Although the CDIS provides data only on FDI stock, RBI's census provides additional data covering some aspects of the functioning of a subset of FDI companies operating in India, namely the subsidiaries of foreign companies. This data is analysed in the following section.

Annual Census on Foreign Liabilities and Assets of Indian Companies

The census provides data regarding the size of operations of subsidiaries of foreign companies across major sectors of the economy (Table 6.1). In 2012–13, just less than two-thirds of the sales of these companies belonged to the manufacturing sector. However, the subsequent years witnessed a steep fall in the share of this sector; in 2017–18, manufacturing companies accounted

Table 6.1: Sales of Foreign Subsidiaries, 2012–18 (Rs Billion)

Activities	*2012–13*	*2013–14*	*2014–15*	*2015–16*	*2016–17*	*2017–18*
A. Agriculture-related, plantations and allied activities	43.7	51.2	64.5	52.9	76.4	72.2
B. Mining	148.3	116.9	113.0	107.3	104.6	126.7
C. Manufacturing	7,307.7	9,757.6	10,207.5	9,041.9	11,058.7	11,879.7
D. Electricity, gas, steam and air-conditioning supply	72	38.1	42.1	144.6	107.9	141.4
E. Water supply, sewerage, waste management and remediation activities	9.9	9.4	6.7	11.1	162.3	185.1
F. Construction	223.1	273.4	247.9	193.1	215.3	223.1
G. Services	3,659.2	5,014.0	5,908.7	6,731.0	8,542.5	10,041.0
Total	11,463.9	15,260.6	16,590.4	16,281.9	20,267.7	22,669.2
Number of foreign subsidiaries included	6,144	7,485	8,032	8,326	8,557	10,215

Source: Annual Census on Foreign Liabilities and Assets of Indian Companies, various years, RBI, available at https://m.rbi.org.in/Scripts/AnnualPublications.aspx?head=Annual%20Census%20on%20Foreign%20Liabilities%20and%20Assets%20of%20Indian%20Companies# (accessed 19 August 2018).

for just a little more than half of the total sales of subsidiaries of foreign companies. The growth of foreign subsidiaries in the services sector is more impressive in absolute terms. In the period for which the data is provided in Table 6.1, sales of the services sector companies grew nearly three-fold, as against a 60 per cent expansion in sales of the manufacturing sector companies. Another important indicator of the ascendancy of services sector companies was that in 2017–18, the number of firms belonging to this sector was more than twice of those engaged in manufacturing. These figures are consistent with our earlier findings about the sectoral inflows of FDI, namely the growing presence of foreign investors in the services sector.

In the manufacturing sector, motor vehicles, trailers and semi-trailers accounted for nearly a fourth of the total sales of the sector in 2017–18, while information and communication service companies contributed to nearly half of the services sector sales. Companies engaged in wholesale and retail trade gained in importance, accounting for over 30 per cent of the services sector sales.

Data on foreign trade of the foreign subsidiaries is presented in Tables 6.2 and 6.3.

Foreign subsidiaries, taken together, ran trade surplus, which was due to the large and growing exports of services. The sectoral patterns mirrored the overall pattern of trade, with the manufacturing and services sector companies recording trade deficit and surplus, respectively.

Exports by foreign subsidiaries increased by over 70 per cent from 2012–13, which was expected given that the share of services sector companies was more than 67 per cent of the total exports. Services exports were driven by the information and communication sectors, accounting for nearly three-fourths of the total exports of this sector, and nearly half of the total exports by all foreign subsidiaries. While foreign subsidiaries engaged in

Table 6.2: Exports of Foreign Subsidiaries, 2012–18 ($ Billion)

Sectors	*2012–13*	*2013–14*	*2014–15*	*2015–16*	*2016–17*	*2017–18*
Manufacturing						
Food products	1.5	6.1	2.9	2.7	1.0	1.0
Coke and refined petroleum products	5.7	6.8	4.5	4.2	0.6	0.7
Chemicals and chemical products	1.6	1.9	1.5	1.4	1.7	1.8
Pharmaceuticals, medicinal and chemical products	1.7	1.8	1.8	1.6	3.1	3.4
Computer, electronic and optical products	3.5	2.7	3.0	2.8	2.4	2.8
Electrical equipment	1.7	1.6	1.7	1.6	1.7	1.5
Machinery and equipment n.e.c.	2.1	2.6	3.6	3.3	2.9	3.3
Motor vehicles, trailers and semi-trailers		6.4	7.1	6.6	8.4	9.5
Total manufacturing	28.3	37.4	40.3	28.1	30.8	34.4
Services						
Wholesale and retail trade, etc.	2.1	2.5	4.3	4.0	5.0	6.7
Transportation and storage	0.9	1.0	1.0	0.9	0.4	0.4
Information and communication	27.8	32.8	42.2	39.4	48.3	55.1
Financial and insurance activities	1.1	1.1	1.6	1.5	1.8	2.2
Total Services	35.6	42.2	48.3	49.6	64.2	74.6
Total for all sectors	64.5	80.1	89.0	78.1	96.0	110.1

Source: Annual Census on Foreign Liabilities and Assets of Indian Companies, various years, RBI, available at https://m.rbi.org.in/Scripts/AnnualPublications.aspx?head=Annual%20Census%20on%20Foreign%20Liabilities%20and%20Assets%20of%20Indian%20Companies# (accessed 19 August 2018).

services increased their exports by more than 70 per cent since 2012–13, those in the manufacturing sector registered a decline in exports after peaking in 2014–15. While there is no discernible trend in the total imports of the manufacturing companies, if the

Table 6.3: Imports of Foreign Subsidiaries, 2012–18 ($ Billion)

Sectors	*2012–13*	*2013–14*	*2014–15*	*2015–16*	*2016–17*	*2017–18*
Manufacturing						
Food products	1.2	10.9	9.6	2.1	2.2	2.2
Coke and refined petroleum products	13.0	12.1	10.1	5.1	0.3	0.6
Chemicals and chemical products	2.1	2.8	3.2	2.5	3.8	4.4
Pharmaceuticals, medicinal and chemical products	1.5	1.3	1.5	1.5	1.9	2.1
Computer, electronic and optical products	3.4	8.8	7.0	8.1	8.0	11.0
Electrical equipment	9.0	2.5	2.6	2.0	3.5	3.8
Machinery and equipment n.e.c.	2.7	1.9	2.3	2.8	3.1	3.6
Motor vehicles, trailers and semi-trailers	1.8	6.3	5.2	4.6	6.0	6.7
Total manufacturing	48.6	57.2	56.0	42.4	44.5	56.4
Services						
Wholesale and retail trade, etc.	7.3	9.0	11.8	10.4	14.0	18.5
Transportation and storage	0.4	0.4	0.5	0.4	0.2	0.2
Information and communication	2.9	3.3	5.0	3.9	5.2	6.3
Financial and insurance activities	0.1	0.1	0.1	0.2	0.2	0.1
Total Services	11.5	13.8	18.5	16.5	20.8	26.9
Total for all sectors	60.9	71.9	75.3	59.8	66.3	84.8

Source: Annual Census on Foreign Liabilities and Assets of Indian Companies, various years, RBI, available at https://m.rbi.org.in/Scripts/AnnualPublications.aspx?head=Annual%20Census%20on%20Foreign%20Liabilities%20and%20Assets%20of%20Indian%20Companies# (accessed 19 August 2018).

imports of coke and refined petroleum products are excluded, there does appear to be a tendency to import more. Many branches of manufacturing increased their imports. The increase was, however, more substantial in case of electronics. Imports by services sector companies also increased substantially, with most of the increase coming from trading companies.

The relative importance of the engagement of foreign subsidiaries in trade can be seen by comparing their exports and imports with their sales and purchases. Tables 6.4 and 6.5 provide the details.

Table 6.4: Share of Exports to Sales, 2012–18

Sectors/Industries	*2012–13*	*2013–14*	*2014–15*	*2015–16*	*2016–17*	*2017–18*
Manufacturing	21.1	23.4	21.8	21.8	19.2	18.6
Food products	20.0	30.9	28.9	28.9	8.3	8.6
Coke and refined petroleum products	33.5	40.0	42.4	42.4	41.5	26.1
Chemicals and chemical products	21.6	13.6	16.9	16.9	18.2	14.3
Pharmaceuticals, medicinal and chemical products	33.4	32.1	32.5	32.5	36.6	44.6
Computer, electronic and optical products	12.4	17.2	19.0	19.0	19.5	15.9
Electrical equipment	23.8	17.1	16.2	16.2	12.9	12.7
Machinery and equipment n.e.c.	18.7	28.6	33.4	33.4	29.5	25.0
Motor vehicles, trailers and semi-trailers	24.8	20.2	20.5	20.5	14.6	20.1
Services	52.9	51.5	48.9	48.9	48.0	47.9
Wholesale and retail trade, etc.	12.3	12.0	15.2	15.2	17.6	14.4
Transportation and storage	33.8	33.9	26.3	26.3	23.7	22.9
Information and communication	78.6	77.2	70.6	70.6	70.0	72.5
Financial and insurance activities	47.0	34.5	32.6	32.6	36.7	37.1

Note: Original figures in Indian rupees converted to US dollars using relevant market exchange rates.

Source: Annual Census on Foreign Liabilities and Assets of Indian Companies, various years, RBI, available at https://m.rbi.org.in/Scripts/AnnualPublications.aspx?head=Annual%20Census%20on%20Foreign%20Liabilities%20and%20Assets%20of%20Indian%20Companies# (accessed 19 August 2018).

Table 6.5: Share of Imports to Purchases, 2012–18

Sectors/Industries	*2012–13*	*2013–14*	*2014–15*	*2015–16*	*2016–17*	*2017–18*
Manufacturing	48.0	50.7	50.6	50.6	43.7	43.9
Food products	23.5	68.2	93.3	93.3	23.3	31.1
Coke and refined petroleum products	79.1	81.5	68.8	68.8	79.2	49.6
Chemicals and chemical products	51.3	46.3	56.2	56.2	51.5	54.5
Pharmaceuticals, medicinal and chemical products	52.5	45.7	50.5	50.5	49.7	54.8
Computer, electronic and optical products	52.7	78.6	85.3	85.3	80.6	88.0
Electrical equipment	79.4	36.4	38.5	38.5	37.6	44.4
Machinery and equipment n.e.c.	38.8	35.6	34.7	34.7	36.7	38.7
Motor vehicles, trailers and semi-trailers	33.2	26.3	23.3	23.3	18.5	19.6
Services	36.3	35.1	30.9	30.9	29.2	31.1
Wholesale and retail trade, etc.	47.0	51.3	48.7	48.7	46.7	47.2
Transportation and storage	25.9	25.1	19.4	19.4	16.9	14.7
Information and communication	30.6	25.4	20.6	20.6	16.9	20.0
Financial and insurance activities	11.5	6.9	17.8	17.8	7.1	6.1

Source: Annual Census on Foreign Liabilities and Assets of Indian Companies, various years, RBI, available at https://m.rbi.org.in/Scripts/AnnualPublications.aspx?head=Annual%20Census%20on%20Foreign%20Liabilities%20and%20Assets%20of%20Indian%20Companies# (accessed 19 August 2018).

Except for the companies in the pharmaceutical industry, foreign subsidiaries operating in India's manufacturing sector had relatively low penetration in international markets. Overall, companies in the manufacturing sector showed declining trends in exports to sales, from close to a quarter of sales in 2012–13 to a fifth in 2017–18. Nearly 45 per cent of the sales of foreign subsidiaries in the pharmaceutical industry were in the international market, which is in keeping with the growing presence of companies based in India in the global markets. In sharp contrast, the electronic and electrical equipment manufacturers had increasingly turned towards the domestic market.

The services sector was relatively more export-oriented; nearly half of their sales were in international markets. Besides companies in the information and communication sectors, finance and insurance companies also had significant exposure to the international markets in 2012–13; however, in the subsequent years, the exports to sales ratio declined.

Imports had a significant share in the purchases of foreign subsidiaries in manufacturing. The import to purchases ratio across the sub-sectors speaks of the extent of their respective import-dependence. For instance, for the electronics industry, imports accounted for 88 per cent of their purchases. Chemicals and pharmaceuticals industries also had large import-dependence, the latter turning to China for their requirements of active pharmaceutical ingredients for producing formulations.

The trends in exports and imports of the foreign subsidiaries in the manufacturing sector companies show that these companies could have played only a marginal role in the regional value chains. In several industries, the companies were sourcing their purchases from international markets, but their sales were clearly domestic market-oriented. There is, therefore, some evidence to suggest that foreign subsidiaries were, by and large, not supporting one of the core objectives of Government of India to make India a hub for manufacturing exports.

Analysis based on Annual Reports of FDI Companies

We analysed the performance of 265 FDI companies using the data available from their annual reports for two years for which consistent data is available. The selected companies belong to five industries, namely auto-ancillaries, automobiles, domestic appliances, pharmaceuticals and electronics. The process of identifying these companies is explained in Appendix 6.1.

Our analysis includes four facets of the FDI companies, which are: trade transactions, payments in foreign exchange on account of dividends as well as royalty, and spending on research and development.

Export intensities of the selected companies, clustered according to their main activities, are provided in Table 6.6.

Table 6.6: Export Intensity of Sample FDI Companies in Select Sectors, 2013–14 to 2014–15

Industries	*No. of Companies*	*Exports of Goods and Services ($ Billion)*	*Total Sales ($ Billion)*	*Share of Exports in Total Sales (%)*
Auto ancillaries	174	1,703.6	17,654.4	9.6
Automobile	13	3,842.0	23,293.6	16.5
Domestic appliances	13	359.2	4,587.8	7.8
Pharmaceuticals	28	2,015.0	4,226.4	47.7
Electronics	37	1,476.0	11,693.8	12.6
All industries	265	9,395.8	61,456.1	15.3

Source: Based on data collected from Prowess and/or company annual reports downloaded from the website of the Ministry of Corporate Affairs, Government of India.

Except for the companies in the pharmaceutical industry, FDI companies had relatively low exposure to the international market. As in the case of the foreign subsidiaries, the set of 265 companies also showed the large participation of the pharmaceutical industry in global markets.

As compared to their export intensities, import intensities of the sample companies was significantly higher (Table 6.7).

FDI companies in the electronics industry had the highest import intensities, which is expected, given the regional/global

Table 6.7: Import Intensity of Sample FDI Companies in Select Sectors, 2013–14 to 2014–15

Industries	*No. of Companies*	*Imports ($ Million)*	*Total Sales ($ Million)*	*Share of Imports in Total Sales (%)*
Auto ancillaries	174	3,251.5	17,654.4	18.4
Automobile	13	3,993.0	23,293.6	17.1
Domestic appliances	13	940.9	4,587.8	20.5
Pharmaceuticals	28	1,111.7	4,226.4	26.3
Electronics	37	5,491.5	11,693.8	47.0
All industries	265	14,788.6	61,456.1	24.1

Source: Based on data collected from Prowess and/or company annual reports downloaded from the website of the Ministry of Corporate Affairs, Government of India.

sourcing of the parts and components by this industry. The degree of import-dependence shown by this smaller sample of companies is much lower than that shown by the subsidiaries of the foreign companies, as reported by the RBI. In case of subsidiaries, however, the import intensities were with respect to *purchases*.

Net foreign exchange earnings of the sample companies are given in the Table 6.8. Expectedly, all industries, barring pharmaceuticals, show net outflows of foreign exchange. The 37 FDI companies belonging to the electronics industry were the highest net spenders of foreign exchange, including on the invisibles account, which include dividends outgo.

Earlier, contribution of FDI companies in the area of technology could be assessed in terms of their research and development (R&D) intensities and through transfer of technologies. While the former indicator can be assessed to the extent that the companies report their R&D activities, the latter can partly be gauged by analysing the royalty and lumpsum payments, which arise from the use of proprietary technologies and/or other forms of intellectual property rights, like trademarks, copyrights and designs.

Table 6.8: Net Earnings in Foreign Exchange, 2013–14 to 2014–15 ($ Million)

Industries	*No. of Companies*	*Exports*	*Imports*	*Trade Balance*	*Other Balances*	*Net Earnings*
Auto ancillaries	174	1,703.6	3,251.5	–1,547.9	–633.7	–2,181.6
Automobile manufacturers	13	3,842.0	3,993.0	–151.0	–1,090.9	–1,241.9
Domestic appliances	13	359.2	940.9	–581.8	–600.8	–1,182.6
Pharmaceuticals	28	2,015.0	1,111.7	903.4	–281.7	621.7
Electronics	37	1,476.0	5,491.5	–4,015.5	–268.1	–4,283.6
All industries	265	9,395.8	14,788.6	–5,392.8	–2,875.2	–8,268.0

Source: Based on data collected from Prowess and/or company annual reports downloaded from the website of the Ministry of Corporate Affairs, Government of India.

Table 6.9 gives some indications about the R&D intensities of the sample FDI companies.

Table 6.9: R&D Intensities of Sample FDI Companies, 2013–14 to 2014–15

Industries	*No. of Companies*	*Sales Turnover ($ Million)*	*R&D Spending ($ Million)*	*R&D Intensities (%)*
Auto ancillaries	174	17,654.4	119.5	0.7
Automobile manufacturers	13	23,293.6	223.6	1.0
Domestic appliances	13	4,587.8	24.3	0.5
Pharmaceuticals	28	4,226.4	122.8	2.9
Electronics	37	11,693.8	8.1	0.1
All industries	265	61,456.1	498.2	0.8

Source: Based on data collected from Prowess and/or company annual reports downloaded from the website of the Ministry of Corporate Affairs, Government of India.

The FDI companies in the sample had low spending on R&D, except for those in the pharmaceutical industry. The most surprising figures are for the 37 companies from the electronics industry included in the sample, which, despite being in one of the technology-intensive areas, spent a negligible amount on R&D.

Table 6.10 helps in making a better assessment of the R&D intensity of the sample companies.

Table 6.10: Detailed Break-up of R&D Intensity, 2013–14 to 2014–15

Range (%)	*Auto Ancillaries*	*Automobile Manufacturers*	*Domestic Appliances*	*Pharma-ceuticals*	*Electronics*	*All Industries*
Nil	106	4	3	13	30	156
Less than 0.1	10		1	4	1	16
0.1 to 0.5	18	3	6	2	2	31
0.5 to 1.0	20		2	2	1	25
1.0 to 2.0	13	4	1	3	3	24
2.0 and above	7	2	—	4	—	13
Grand total	174	13	13	28	37	265

Source: Based on data collected from Prowess and/or company annual reports downloaded from the website of the Ministry of Corporate Affairs, Government of India.

Table 6.10 shows that of the 265 companies, 156 (or nearly 60 per cent of the total) did not conduct any R&D. A further 72 companies had R&D intensity of 1 per cent or less, levels that are sub-optimal. Only 13 companies had R&D intensity of 2 per cent or more; these are the only companies that have some potential to conduct meaningful research. FDI companies can, therefore, make at most a very minor contribution towards the strengthening of the technological base of India's manufacturing sector.

Royalty payments by FDI companies are indicators of their use of intellectual property like patents, trademarks and copyrighted proprietary technologies owned by their parents, affiliates or other companies. These payments can be interpreted in two very different ways: one, they may be seen as indicators of infusion of foreign technologies, and two, they can be interpreted as technological dependence, if royalty payments are continuously made. Royalty payments are an important source of extraction of economic rent by the owners of intellectual property, and such payments can become a source of economic drain, if they persist over long periods.

India has seen growing concern regarding royalty payments because of a steep increase in such payments in recent years. RBI has reported that during the past decade, payments to owners of intellectual property have increased nearly seven-fold, from about \$1 billion to \$7 billion (Figure 6.1). The rate of increase remained unabated in 2018–19; in the first six months of that year, the payments crossed \$4 billion. It may be mentioned here that the government had removed the limits on royalty payments in 2009.[3]

Figure 6.1: Charges for the Use of Intellectual Property, 2007–18

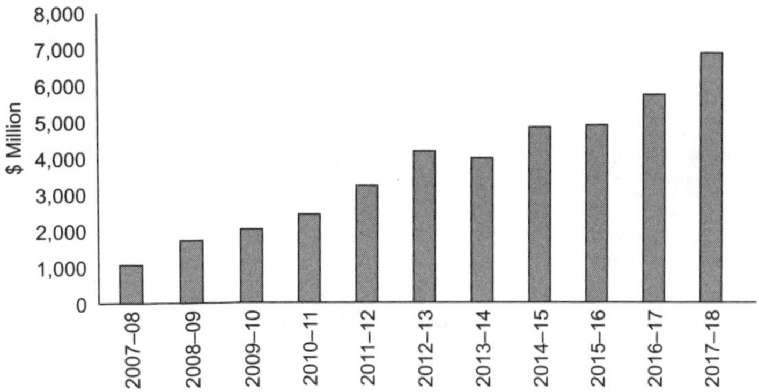

Source: *Handbook of Statistics on Indian Economy*, various years, RBI, available at https://www.rbi.org.in/Scripts/AnnualPublications.aspx?head=Handbook%20of%20Statistics%20on%20Indian%20Economy (accessed 21 August 2018).

In this context, it would be useful to consider the royalty payments made by large FDI companies in recent years. In many of these companies, especially in Microsoft, Samsung, Hyundai and Hindustan Unilever, royalty payments increased significantly. Aggregate payments by these companies increased by 76 per cent during 2013–14 to 2017–18. The payments in 2017–18 were, in fact, double of those in 2012–13 (Table 6.11).

Table 6.11: Estimated Royalty Payments by Select FDI Companies, 2012–18 ($ Million)

FDI Companies	*2012–13*	*2013–14*	*2014–15*	*2015–16*	*2016–17*	*2017–18*	*Total*
Maruti Suzuki India Ltd	484.0	436.7	479.4	530.2	583.7	620.6	3,134.6
Microsoft Corporation (India) Pvt. Ltd	0.4	166.4	270.8	392.3	523.8	551.8	1,905.5
Oracle India Pvt. Ltd	270.2	261.4	318.5	295.8	368.5	404.2	1,918.6
Samsung India Electronics Pvt. Ltd	54.4	89.1	237.9	293.6	374.6	398.6	1,448.2
Sap India Pvt. Ltd	185.0	176.6	184.1	198.9	237.5	261.8	1,243.9
Hyundai Motor India Ltd	79.3	77.7	118.0	138.4	143.0	158.0	714.4
Hindustan Unilever Ltd	68.3	84.3	116.4	130.6	101.6	100.4	601.6
Honda Cars India Ltd	50.6	75.1	114.2	93.5	83.5	90.3	507.2
Toyota Kirloskar Motor Pvt. Ltd	58.5	59.0	63.2	57.0	99.3	103.1	440.1
Renault Nissan Automotive India Pvt. Ltd	30.8	41.9	79.9	68.5	82.0	65.9	369.0
Nokia Solutions & Networks India Pvt. Ltd	16.2	54.0	72.0	114.9	11.6	49.5	318.2
Nestle India Ltd	52.8	49.9	56.0	45.6	53.3	65.0	322.6
ABB India Ltd	43.9	41.5	42.4	56.4	54.5	59.5	298.2
Procter & Gamble Home Products Pvt. Ltd	35.9	35.6	39.8	35.8	33.3	36.8	217.2
Ford India Pvt. Ltd	17.0	15.2	21.5	48.0	74.5	75.9	252.1
JCB India Ltd	37.2	30.4	26.2	31.2	42.0	76.8	243.8
Reckitt Benckiser (India) Pvt. Ltd	28.1	28.2	29.1	31.6	36.1	37.6	190.7
LG Electronics India Pvt. Ltd	28.9	27.3	30.0	29.2	32.6	36.4	184.4

(Contd)

Table 6.11 (Contd)

FDI Companies	*2012–13*	*2013–14*	*2014–15*	*2015–16*	*2016–17*	*2017–18*	*Total*
Colgate-Palmolive (India) Ltd	26.4	27.2	30.1	29.4	27.4	28.8	169.3
Dassault Systems India Pvt. Ltd	N.R.	29.5	30.6	33.6	40.2	40.7	174.6
John Deere India Pvt. Ltd	21.3	27.0	26.1	29.4	29.6	25.4	158.8
Bosch Ltd	27.0	22.0	29.8	23.9	24.9	32.5	160.1
IBM India Pvt. Ltd	28.5	24.6	23.1	23.4	25.5	25.0	150.1
GlaxoSmithKline Consumer Healthcare Ltd	20.1	26.6	23.0	23.1	22.2	22.1	137.1
Total	1,664.6	1,907.3	2,461.8	2,754.3	3,095.0	3,366.7	14,486.9

Source: Prowess database and Annual Reports of Companies. Converted from the corresponding rupee values using the rates applied by Prowess.

Appendix 6.1: Selection of Companies

Researchers face many, and most often, insurmountable obstacles in studying the Indian corporate sector. Given that an overwhelming part of the FDI is invested in companies registered under the Companies Act, studies of their role and place in the economy also suffer from the limitations of the system. Studies about the impact of FDI are generally based on identifying small sets of companies selected from popular corporate databases like Prowess from the Centre for Monitoring Indian Economy (CMIE), and Capitaline. Given the major differences in the characteristics of foreign investors described in the foregoing discussion, the sectors invested in and the modes of entry (for example, M&A *versus* greenfield), it is obvious that observed relationships based on the aggregates can never be robust.

These popular databases are primarily focused on the companies listed on the stock exchange. While they do include other companies, their inclusion does not follow any systematic procedure. Even though corporate filings have been made in electronic form for some years now, the system is, so far, not geared to respond to analysis of many of the critical attributes of the sector. Changes in the reporting format have compounded the problem further, and made locating relevant data in the filings, and making comparisons over time, increasingly difficult.

For a long time, transactions in foreign exchange were reported in a set format under clearly identifiable categories. The main items of expenditure in foreign exchange were exports and imports, receipts and payments on account of dividends, royalty, know-how, professional and consultancy fees, and interest. This vital information, however, finds no place in the new format. While companies are required to report earnings and expenditure in foreign exchange in the report of the board of directors, they do not follow any standard pattern.

This was the background in which we had to carry out the exercise of tracing performance indicators of FDI companies included in the earlier discussion. Of the 1,480 companies classified under the selected industries and each having at least $1 million total income during 2013–14, the Prowess database identified 126 companies as having foreign equity holdings.

In view of the inconsistencies in the reporting of data, especially of transactions in foreign exchange described earlier, it was also decided to reconfirm in case of missing entries. Company classification was also rechecked by referring to publicly available shareholding patterns of listed companies, and annual reports downloaded from the website of the Ministry of Corporate Affairs.

Following this exercise, several companies were included as FDI companies, while some others had to be dropped because the relevant details were missing. Gaps regarding royalty payments were filled using the information available in the company annual reports, directly or as part of the disclosures under related party transactions.

This exercise helped us identify 265 FDI companies with *reasonably reliable data* on indicators used in the foregoing discussion.

Notes

1. Companies registered with the Ministry of Corporate Affairs are required to submit their annual reports.

2. Prowess is a database of the financial performance of companies. Annual reports of companies, stock exchanges and regulators are the principal sources of the data. The database is produced by the Centre for Monitoring Indian Economy (CMIE).

3. Before 2009, payment of royalties under foreign technology collaboration did not require government approval as long as the payment was up to $2 million and the royalty payments were 5 per cent of domestic sales and 8 per cent of export values. The Liberalisation of Foreign Technology Agreement policy, notified by Press Note No. 8 of 2009, removed this cap.

Reference

IMF. 2015. 'Coordinated Direct Investment Survey Guide'. Washington, D. C.

seven
Summary and Conclusions

This book has been written with two objectives. One, to situate FDI in the development discourse in the post-colonisation period by explaining the evolution of FDI from the early 1950s, and to thereby understand the characteristics of an important component of North–South financial flows. Alongside this narrative, we have also given a perspective on the functioning of the organisational manifestation of FDI, namely the TNCs. The second objective was to discuss and discover India's tryst with FDI during the phase when successive governments invited FDI to be a partner in the country's progress.

In the early years of the post-colonisation phase, covering the 1950s, developing countries had a somewhat divided opinion about this source of finance. While these countries themselves recognised that FDI may be useful for financing their developmental needs, several scholars writing in this period commented on the exploitative character of the foreign companies, which could stymie the progress of these countries. On the other hand, the main source of FDI in these years, the US, was actively engaged in encouraging its private investors from investing abroad, including in the then underdeveloped regions of the world.

The trend was thus set for FDI to be closely linked to the directions provided by the largest creditor country, the US. In the 1950s, the US government was keen to maximise the returns to capital when it was running a surplus on its current account, but in the following decade, it turned against American companies investing abroad when its economy began leaking capital. Desperate to prevent the loss of confidence in the dollar and, therefore, its hegemonic role in the Bretton Woods system, the US imposed controls on FDI. Thus, began a phase of relative decline of FDI in the global capital markets, a trend that was exacerbated in the 1970s, when private capital, particularly bank finance, became the dominant form of international capital flows.

FDI gained ground following the developing-country debt crisis in the 1980s, when it was involved in buying out debts of the heavily indebted developing countries in a number of swap deals. This led to its emergence as a key element in the framework of economic reforms of developing countries, more commonly known as the Washington Consensus, promoted by the World Bank and IMF. As part of this framework, developing countries, which had earlier followed a regulated regime for FDI, began pursuing open-door policies.

One of the important elements of this book has been the discussion on the evolution of the concept of FDI. We pointed out that the definition of FDI, or how direct investment companies are identified, has changed several times over the past many decades. The common understanding of FDI is that this form of capital exerts control or a significant degree of influence over the enterprise it invests in the host country. This is the distinct feature of FDI, one that sets it apart from portfolio investment. 'Control' was seen to be exercised through the ownership of equity capital or voting shares of the direct investment enterprise. The link between ownership and control was established in the US, where 25 per cent or more of the equity capital owned by a foreign enterprise was identified as direct investment. The IMF, too, recognised that 'ownership of 25 per cent of the voting stock by a closely organised group of non-residents, may be taken as evidence of direct control' (IMF 1961: paragraph 373).

In subsequent decades, two significant changes were introduced for the purposes of identifying a direct investment enterprise. This revised template for identifying FDI was given by the OECD in 1983 (IMF 1992: 24) and later endorsed by the IMF in BPM5 (IMF 1993: 86). First, the extent of foreign ownership deemed necessary for exercising control over an enterprise was reduced from the earlier 25 per cent to 10 per cent of equity capital of an enterprise. Second, other than foreign investments in equity capital for setting up enterprises, FDI now included two other funding mechanisms used by the foreign investors in their host countries. These were reinvested earnings of existing direct investment enterprises and inter-corporate loans.

FDI flows entered a new trajectory of expansion from the 1990s, after developing countries embraced the policies of economic liberalisation. The real expansion of FDI took place from the beginning of the new millennium, when average annual inflows for the decade of the 2000s crossed the $1.5-trillion mark. The financial crisis in the closing years of the decade impacted the inflows, but once the capital markets overcame crisis mode, inflows got their momentum back. In the first seven years of this millennium, average annual inflows got closer to the $3-trillion mark. However, there are indications that FDI inflows have declined in 2017, largely on account of a dip in inflows into the developed country regions.

An interesting tendency seen in the total foreign investment inflows, which includes FDI, portfolio investments and other investment inflows, including derivatives, is that until the current decade, FPI had the largest share in the inflows. This tendency has been reversed in the decade of the 2010s, with FDI topping portfolio investments. What could explain this phenomenon? One likely explanation is that since the previous decade, a larger number of developing countries have adopted the OECD–IMF definition of FDI; for instance, India formally adopted the methodology in the early years of the 2000s. But it is also a fact that authorities in many jurisdictions do not strictly adhere to the OECD–IMF methodology and, therefore, count most foreign investments (including portfolio investments) as FDI. This feature of FDI statistics is a major lacuna in understanding the real importance of FDI in today's economic dynamics.

India's Tryst with FDI

India's tryst with FDI began immediately after the country attained political independence. Starting with the statement of Prime Minister Nehru on foreign investments in 1949, to the adoption of the Industrial Policy Resolution in 1956, Government of India gave foreign investors the opportunities to participate in the country's industrialisation. In subsequent decades, several key policies on FDI, including the controversial FERA of 1973, performed the important task of defining the scope of foreign investment, thereby lending a sense of predictability to the foreign investors. Not surprisingly, many companies with significantly high levels of foreign participation in equity capital expanded after FERA was included in the statute book.

Over the two decades spanning the 2000s and 2010s, India has emerged as one of the most attractive destinations for FDI. This is the outcome of a complete turnaround in the policies governing FDI, which changed from mildly encouraging foreign investors in earlier decades to warm embrace from the mid-1990s.

By the government's own admission, India has one of the most foreign investor-friendly policies in the world (Government of India 2017b).

The first signs of this metamorphosis of India's FDI policy came with the unveiling of the IPS almost immediately after the economic liberalisation policies were introduced in 1991. This statement spoke of FDI as the key agent of change; the government expected that foreign investors would help overcome the lack of dynamism in India's manufacturing sector. The tone of the government policies *vis-à-vis* FDI which was set in the 1990s reverberates even more in many of the key policy pronouncements of the successive governments.

In an attempt to revive the manufacturing sector in the previous decade, the then government took far-reaching steps to invite FDI into India. Foreign investors were increasingly allowed to enter without even minimal review, reversing the earlier policy of subjecting these investors to a limited review, with a few exceptions, before they could bring in their funds. The limited review, which was essentially in the nature of oversight functions, was performed by the FIPB, established after the announcement of the IPS of 1991. Having progressively diluted the FIPB, Government of India finally decided to dismantle the organisation in 2017 (Government of India 2017a: paragraph 96).

The sectors in which FDI was positioned as a critical element for their upgradation and development, by successive governments in the 2010s, included defence and retail. Thus, restrictions on the entry of FDI into the defence sector were progressively relaxed, eventually rendering this sector of strategic importance as one of those most open to FDI. A similar roadmap was laid out for the retail sector, but in the crucial sub-sector of multi-brand retail, stakeholder opposition stymied the entry of foreign firms.

Understanding and Interpreting India's Inflows

The success of the 'Make in India' initiative, the most ambitious programme, adopted in 2014, to modernise the manufacturing, services and infrastructure sectors, was also predicated on substantial inflows of FDI. Similar was the thrust of another proposed policy initiative, the 'Industrial Policy'; FDI was given a key role in the implementation of this policy as well, so much so that despite expressing dissatisfaction over FDI's contribution, it proposed to attract $100 billion annually.

Since the 1990s, therefore, Government of India has consistently signalled that it is almost completely dependent on FDI for making the country's manufacturing and services sectors globally competitive. Do we have evidence that foreign investors have responded to the government's priorities?

Assessing the response of foreign investors to the policy changes brought by the government is a daunting task, largely because the database provided by the two official agencies, namely the RBI and DPIIT, have a number of limitations. In the 1990s, FDI data initially comprised only equity investments made by foreign investors. And from 2000–01, the coverage of FDI was expanded to include, in addition to equity capital, retained earnings of FDI companies (reinvested earnings) and 'other direct capital' (inter-corporate debt transactions between related parties, in other words, between direct investors, and subsidiary branches and associates). Data on equity capital includes equity of incorporated as well as unincorporated entities. These changes were introduced in keeping with the OECD–IMF definition of FDI. With the official agencies frequently changing the criteria for identifying FDI and the reporting format, inter-temporal comparisons are a difficult task.

But the more problematic aspect of the available FDI data is that although the RBI spoke of presenting the data in accordance with 'international best practice', the organisation has also informed subsequently that the present definition being used to classify FDI in India is at variance with the OECD–IMF definition, which recommends 10 per cent as the share in equity holding for defining FDI. The threshold limit of 10 per cent is not strictly adhered to, clarifies the RBI. This clarification is very significant, for it lays bare one of the fundamental problems with India's FDI data, namely that the distinction between direct and portfolio investment can be, at best, fuzzy.

The regulatory mechanism for foreign companies, existing prior to 1991, could lie at the root of this problem. Under this mechanism, the participation of foreign companies could be in two forms: foreign financial collaboration and foreign technical collaboration. Foreign investments routed through financial collaborations were recorded, and the extent of foreign participations in total equity of existing or proposed companies registered in India was not usually clarified. This manner of capturing the financial contribution of foreign companies in existing or proposed Indian companies has continued even after the change in the definition of FDI was officially incorporated from 2000–01. Our analysis of FDI inflows, too, was based on this less-than-perfect database.

FDI inflows into India expanded rapidly after the mid-1990s, reaching $3.5 billion in 1997–98, just as the east Asian financial crisis was taking the global capital markets downhill. This data informs us that fuels and telecommunications were the two sectors that the foreign investors favoured; these sectors accounted for more than 60 per cent of the total investment that the government had approved. The sources from which India was receiving inflows were diverse in the early years of the 1990s, but in the later years, the share of tax havens like Mauritius increased.

These two characteristics of FDI inflows in the 1990s, namely the larger share of the non-manufacturing sectors and the dominance of tax havens, could be seen in the subsequent phases as well.

The adoption of the international best practice and inclusion of the additional categories of funds invested by foreign investors did result in an increase in the reported FDI inflows, but it was only in 2004–05, that they were distinctly higher than the levels reached in the earlier decade. In the following years, FDI inflows went up to $22 billion in 2006–07 and then further to $42 billion in 2008–09, even when the global capital markets were facing one of the worst crises.

Sectoral inflows in this period were skewed towards the services sector, a trend that would remain in the following decade as well. Although the government of the day began emphasising on the need to revive the manufacturing sector, direct investors did not respond adequately. This trend repeated itself even when the government, in 2014, introduced the most ambitious policy focused on the manufacturing sector in nearly six decades since the announcement of the Industrial Policy Resolution in 1956.

Identified tax havens were the main sources of FDI. These countries continued to channelise funds to major economies like India, even when the OECD and the Group of Twenty (G-20) countries were engaged in developing mechanisms to limit their stranglehold over global capital markets. This practice not only indicates the possible loss of tax revenues, it also prevents assessing the host-country responses to India's efforts at attracting FDI.

Quality of the Inflows

In the 2010s, FDI inflows into India reached record levels, going beyond $60 billion. The country had leap-frogged to a position among the group of countries which, from the point of view of the foreign investors, were attractive destinations. However, serious questions about the utility and reliability of these inflows are beginning to surface. Our detailed research into the essential character of the FDI inflows into India has shown that only about half of the inflows could qualify as real-FDI, that is, they could potentially be the providers of the 'package of development inputs', the critical intangibles like technology and managerial skills, besides capital. This finding is consistent with the fact that the RBI, following the international best practice, does not identify if the intra- and inter-corporate investments coming from abroad are indeed FDI.

A second worrisome territory that FDI has entered in recent years is divestment or repatriation of capital. In 2017–18, divestment was almost a third of the total inflows, and nearly half of the equity inflows for the year. This implies that there has been a sharp erosion in the net inflows of FDI.

Even if Indian policymakers were aware of the meaning and purpose of caps on foreign shareholding, it did not get reflected in the way the caps were implemented. Further, progressive dilution of the caps leaves one wondering what objectives the caps were expected to serve. This was more so when the possibilities of further diluting the FDI policy with respect to the manufacturing sector were practically exhausted after 2000. Categorisation of foreign investments for policy purposes (as distinct from statistical purposes), and the way indirect FDI was defined, further suggest that they were driven by short-term exigencies rather than being the result of a well-designed strategy.

Analyses of participation of FDI in the Indian economy showed that there were at least two counts on which the country was not able to secure long-term benefits. First, official data on approvals of FDI proposals up to 2001, and those on actual FDI inflows for the subsequent period, showed that foreign investors preferred investing especially in the services sectors. However, the focus of the government's policy was on attracting FDI for reviving the manufacturing sector, which is an important development objective. Second, India started looking for FDI to meet the CAD instead of its other specific attributes, especially technology for upgrading the productive sectors to make them competitive. Growing disinvestments could be directly related to the major involvement of financial investors and the role of M&As. The non-specific and liberal definition of FDI and its active promotion by the international agencies are at the root of this problem.

India's experience of FDI inflows since the 1990s can perhaps be summed-up as follows: the State treated these inflows as their partners to provide competitive strengths to the productive sectors and, therefore, offered them concessions, but the foreign investors were more interested in extracting the concessions from the State without being the true partners of the kind that the Indian State needed.

References

Government of India. 2017a. 'Budget 2017–2018: Speech of Arun Jaitley, Minister of Finance'. 1 February.

_____. 2017b. 'Foreign Direct Investment Inflows: A Success Story'. Ministry of Commerce and Industry, 19 May. Available at https://pib.gov.in/PressReleseDetail.aspx?PRID=1490278 (accessed 12 May 2018).

IMF. 1961. 'Balance of Payments Manual', third edition. Washington, D. C.

_____. 1992. 'Report on the Measurement of International Capital Flows'. Washington, D. C.

_____. 1993. 'Balance of Payments Manual', fifth edition. Washington, D. C.

Annexure: Tax Havens Identified by the European Union (EU) and Oxfam

Oxfam	*EU's Blacklist*	*EU's Greylist*	
Albania	American Samoa	Albania	Malaysia
Anguilla	Bahrain	Andorra	Maldives
Antigua and Barbuda	Barbados	Armenia	Mauritius
Bahamas	Grenada	Aruba	Montenegro
British Virgin Islands*	Guam	Belize	Morocco
Cook Islands	Korea (Republic of)	Bermuda	Nauru
Gibraltar	Macao SAR	Bosnia	New Caledonia
Jersey	Marshall Islands	Botswana	Niue
Singapore	Mongolia	Cabo Verde	Oman
US Virgin Islands	Namibia	Cayman Islands	Peru
	Palau	Cook Islands	Qatar
	Panama	Curaçao	Saint Vincent
	Saint Lucia	Faroe Islands	San Marino
	Samoa	Fiji	Serbia
	Trinidad and Tobago	Former Yugoslav Republic of Macedonia	Seychelles
	Tunisia	Greenland	Swaziland
	United Arab Emirates	Guernsey	Switzerland
		Herzegovina	Taiwan
		Hong Kong SAR	Thailand
		Isle of Man	The Grenadines
		Jamaica	Turkey
		Jersey	Uruguay
		Jordan	Vanuatu
		Labuan Island	Vietnam
		Liechtenstein	

Note: * Indicates that the jurisdiction has been identified as a conduit tax haven.

Sources: Oxfam, 'Blacklist or Whitewash?: What a Real EU Blacklist of Tax Havens Should Look Like', 27 November 2017, available at https://www.oxfam.org/en/research/blacklist-or-whitewash-what-real-eu-blacklist-tax-havens-should-look (accessed 5 September 2018); Council of the European Union, 'The EU List of Non-cooperative Jurisdictions for Tax Purposes', ECOFIN 1088, 5 December 2017.